Stop
Struggling

the how-to of personal change

by Rita Spencer and
Angela Rossmanith

Angus&Robertson
An imprint of HarperCollins*Publishers*

Angus & Robertson
An imprint of HarperCollins*Publishers* (Australia) Pty Ltd
(ACN 008 431 730)

HarperCollins*Publishers*
25 Ryde Road Pymble, Sydney NSW 2073
22–24 Joseph Street North Blackburn, Melbourne VIC 3130
31 View Road, Auckland 10, New Zealand

First published 1995
Designed by Rosemarie Franzoni
Cover design by Rosemarie Franzoni
Cover illustration by Neryl Walker

Typeset in Gill Sans and Garamond by J&M Typesetting
Printed in Australia by Griffin Paperbacks

The National Library of Australia
Cataloguing-in-Publication data:

Spencer, Rita.
  Stop struggling: the how-to of personal change.

  ISBN 0 207 18903 X (pbk.).

  1. Personality change. 2. Self-realization. 3. Self-help
  techniques. 4. Attitude change. I. Rossmanith, Angela.
  II. Title.

158.1

CONTENTS

Preface

We have used both the masculine and the feminine gender throughout Part One. The case studies in the book reflect the proportion of men to women who have done the course on which this material is based. We have used mainly the feminine gender throughout Parts Three and Four because to alternate between genders in these workbook sections would have caused inevitable confusion to the reader.

No case study is based entirely on any one person or family, but each represents some of the most frequently encountered situations, problems and personality types. If any of the characteristics in these case studies seems familiar, the coincidence is, of course, intentional.

The ideas, procedures and suggestions contained in this book are not intended as a substitute for consulting with a physician, psychiatrist, therapist or clinical psychologist.

Dedication

To the brave pioneers of the ultimate frontier — inner space — and especially to the teachers, thinkers and writers of the eighties. You dared to be different; you didn't wait on certainty; you made some mistakes; you gave so many so much; you took great risks; you taught us well. We acknowledge your contribution to the evolution of our insights into the nature of personal change and the truth about personal reality.

Acknowledgments

I wish to thank all who have taken the course from which this book emerged, for your contribution to the evolution of this material. Special thanks to those of you who have unfailingly been there with enthusiasm, encouragement and personal support, and to Celia for also 'taking up the slack'. I thank my children, Paul and Kari, for sharing my passion for personal growth and for making space for my work in our lives and home. Thanks to my husband John, without whose unconditional love, gourmet meals, computer expertise, secretarial support, and endless cups of tea with wicked cakes, I would be nowhere near where I now am.

Rita Spencer

I thank all my family, and in particular Gunther, Kate, Julia and Luke, for their companionship in, and commitment to, the process of personal change.

Angela Rossmanith

We both thank John Maurer and Helena Cornelius for their professional advice.

PART ONE

Understanding Belief Systems

'I just want to feel better than I often do. You know, more content — and more in control of my life.'

Melissa sounded exasperated. After a moment she leant forward and confided urgently, 'I've tried! I've read self-help books and even done a few courses. But I still don't seem able to make the changes inside myself that I need. The truth is, nothing really changes.'

Her eyes searched the room as though the answer possibly lay hidden among the books on the shelves, or even behind the curtains.

Melissa was in her mid-thirties, articulate and intelligent. She had a steady relationship with her partner, Peter, and together they enjoyed a circle of friends and many shared interests. They had recently purchased a small terrace house which they planned to renovate.

Melissa worked for a film production company where she was appreciated for her efficiency and competence. To her friends, Melissa's life seemed like a dream, but as she put it, 'It is a dream that I can see I am going to destroy with my own dissatisfaction'.

The anxious woman now sitting in the chair fighting back tears of frustration and confusion was light years away from the Melissa most people knew.

'I know I've got lots to be thankful for, but something's just not right, and if I go on like this then the future looks terribly gloomy. Is it asking too much to want to be happy? When I look around at other people — the people at work, let's say — they seem to just get on with their lives. It's as if they've been given a book of rules on how to be happy and somehow I've missed out.'

> Melissa was right in a way: every one of us does have a 'book of
> rules' by which we live life, although perhaps an inner computer
> program is a more apt analogy. This inner program is a system of
> beliefs which basically comprise our personality.

Our inner programming

Each of us, when we were very young, formed a variety of beliefs
about ourselves and about life; beliefs that are both positive and
negative. For example:

It's easy for me to make friends.

I'm not very creative.

I am capable and efficient.

I have to achieve to be valued.

The positive beliefs have enabled us to achieve all the good things
we have in our lives to date but, as adults, we are often unaware of
many of the more negative, limiting beliefs we hold which are the
primary cause of our suffering. Beliefs like:

It's not OK to make mistakes.

Others must come first.

I don't matter much.

Life wasn't meant to be easy/fun/joyful.

Play it safe — never take risks.

I'm really not good enough / nice enough / smart enough / strong
enough.

Like a computer program these beliefs whirr away inside us, many
of them at a subconscious level, powerfully shaping our perceptions,
moulding our attitudes and consequently determining the ways we
act and re-act, the decisions we make, and therefore the ways we feel.

It is the negative aspects of this inner program that trigger negative
emotions like sadness, anxiety and anger. Furthermore, our personal
program leads us to make life choices which prove that program to
be right. In other words, our program becomes a self-fulfilling
prophecy.

One of the most common analogies for our experience of life is that we are on a journey; we are travellers aiming to learn all we can while enjoying ourselves along the way. As pilgrims, we move onwards, stumbling here and there, being helped along by others at particularly difficult times and alone on certain stretches. As we struggle on, we are guided every step of the way by our beliefs program.

Is your program of 'rules' for living life working for you or against you?

Does your program obscure your vision and set you off on routes that do not in fact lead to where you would like to be going?

Has it landed you on a circular road along which you hear the same old sounds and view the same old scenery, day after day?

Has it left you stuck in a rut, or on a dead-end street?

Does it have you dancing to a tune that ends you-know-not-where?

Does it confuse you, so that you find it hard to come to grips with life, to know what you actually do want?

It is the negative or limiting aspects of our individual set of beliefs about ourselves and about the world and how it works that lead to our inner conflicts, lead us to make unwise choices, and lead us to react inappropriately to others.

It is these limiting beliefs that obscure our perception and cause our pain and struggle.

As a result, like Melissa, we may sometimes wonder how we can be happy, whether we will ever enjoy deeply satisfying relationships, how we can lead truly fulfilling lives.

It works this way. We may have learnt, for instance, that 'it is selfish to think about myself' and so have spent life ignoring our own feelings, only to find we have ended up feeling like a doormat. Others will treat us this way if that is the way we treat ourselves. Or we may have taken on a belief like 'I have to achieve to be acceptable' and spent many years running harder and harder up the ladder of success only to find our family complaining that we are not sufficiently available to them and take them for granted — that in their eyes we are indeed 'failing' as a parent and partner.

It seems strange to have to go through life not knowing the contents of the program that drives us, and not knowing how to re-write it as we would now like it to be.

> Melissa was searching for the cause of her dissatisfaction and recognised quickly that she had indeed programmed into her personality some difficult beliefs about herself and about life which were now triggering her feelings of frustration and anxiety, and preventing her from enjoying the good things she did have in life.

How we developed our beliefs program

We all, of course, programmed into ourselves the guidelines passed on to us by parents, guardians, siblings, peer groups, and society at large. This represents the accumulation of programming that was repetitive — the socialisation process — and we are usually aware of the contents of much of this program.

However, the more subtle and pervasive beliefs that are the essence of our individual personalities were programmed largely through our childhood perception of how we had to be in order to get and keep what we most needed — parental love, approval and attention.

These beliefs were largely programmed by us as children and do not therefore constitute a rational program since we either had not reached the age of reason at that time or, at best, were not fully rational adults. These people were principally our parents and as a child it was necessary that we spontaneously adapted to their habits and demands, at an age when we were too young to rationally decide our responses for ourselves. When we are children, adults

> Our beliefs program was put in place by our non-rational childhood responses to people and events.

seem godlike and their words and reactions fall with great weight because we are so dependent on them.

For example, if my parents had constantly told me that 'children should be seen and not heard', I may have internalised a belief that children (including me) are not worthwhile and have nothing to contribute. This belief would then become an integral part of my personality, a core belief about myself. This may or may not have been the message my parents were sending me. It is simply a child's innate response to the particular environment. It is the direct outcome of a young child's feelings and perceptions, unfiltered through the rational adult mind.

Sometimes people are adamant that their own parents were kind, loving and caring, that they did all they could for them and it is impossible to imagine that they have had anything to do with negative programming. The fact is that most parents do the very best they can for their children; we are not suggesting that you regard your parents as monsters who have scarred you for life with their negative messages. But we must keep in mind that small children absorb much of what is in the environment. They are aware and alert, and they can pick up even the slightest tension, as any parent of an infant can verify. As well, there are very few people, if any at all, who have never experienced some self-doubt or any of the negative emotions such as fear, anger or sadness.

It follows that a child may very well sense the sadness of a parent, for example, and, feeling powerless to change that sadness, may feel responsible for it. Very young children do not distinguish between themselves and what is going on around them. Hence they easily feel responsible for events or situations.

More than one person has talked to us about the feelings of inferiority their parents had for a variety of reasons and which they picked up as children. One man, Theo, had devoted parents, as many of us do, yet he still managed to be, in part, negatively programmed. He told us: 'My parents are Greek and were living here at a time when it was definitely not fashionable to be Greek. They carried enormous feelings of shame about where they came from, and tried impossibly hard to be good citizens and to be accepted.

'Now, even though they are elderly, they still defer to others, and it makes me upset to see it. What I am aware of is the sense of shame I picked up, which is at the core of me. It is part of a core belief I have about myself that I am not worthy and I have to struggle to be acceptable. This has affected absolutely everything I've ever done, of course, and I am working on changing it right now.'

The taking on of limiting beliefs is a child's way of adapting to parents' perceived or real demands. This adaptation is essential because a child's survival depends on maintaining parents' love, attention and approval.

> As a child, Melissa often heard the expressions 'Near enough is not good enough' and 'The devil makes work for idle hands', especially from her mother who was constantly busy and insisted on high standards of cleanliness and tidiness. Melissa took on the beliefs that 'I'm only acceptable if I am busy' and 'It's not safe to relax until *everything* is done'. These beliefs kept her running on a treadmill, never being able to appreciate what she had achieved or to take much delight in anything. In her perception there was no time, and besides, to relax and enjoy was to be lazy. She felt constantly frustrated as a result.

Attached to every belief that we have is some usually strong emotion. This is how it works: each limiting belief has associated with it a powerhouse of emotional tension that has steadily built in intensity since first taken on as a belief.

Imagine, for example, a child with an over-protective mother. This child might form all kinds of beliefs as a result, but let's say she takes on the limiting belief 'I'm not capable — I need others to do it for me'. What kinds of emotions might go hand in hand with such a belief and such thinking? Powerlessness? Resentment? Insecurity? Probably all three!

A belief is a thought about reality that is held with strong emotion.

Let's say that the predominant emotion is resentment. The consequent emotions are stored along with the belief and remain for as long as the belief remains. If the belief is a core belief the emotion becomes a core emotion held as an integral part of the personality. It becomes part of who that person (thinks she) is. 'Oh, she's just hopeless — and surly too!' people will say, reinforcing her negative self-image. She says to herself in turn, 'I knew it! Others really are smarter than I am', igniting the consequent emotion of resentment and angry thoughts like 'Well, they should make allowances for me — they shouldn't expect so much of me'.

The child in us

Every one of us has been a child and this child continues to live on in us throughout our lives. This child-within is the container of genuineness, truthfulness and naturalness in each of us, and it is the holder of our early personal history. It is our child-within who cries, who hurts, and who wants to be cared for, nurtured and protected. It is easy to understand this part of ourselves if we turn our eyes and hearts to any outer child.

> The beliefs we took on in childhood are carried still by our child-within who is the part of us that feels and responds emotionally.

It is because we think we have left the child behind, because we think we have grown past the needs of childhood and are independent adults, that life can become difficult. This usually happens because the child in us is crying out for attention and is sad, angry or fearful as a result of being ignored or mistreated by us.

Some of us feel embarrassed at the very idea of part of us still being child-like, but this is the very part of us that holds the key to our future fulfilment and happiness. Our embarrassment is simply the result of some very limiting beliefs we have programmed into ourselves about who we have to be as adults.

Our inner-child then, is our present emotional selves as well as our historical selves. The importance of integrating this inner-child into our lives has long been acknowledged by many psychologists and therapists who recognise that when we can effectively nurture our own inner-child, encouraging her to trust us and to express herself with freedom and ease, not only do we expand our own potential for living fully and with joy, but we enhance our ability to parent our own children. This is because we tend to parent our own children as we parent the inner-child.

How do we nurture our inner-child? By loving her unconditionally — that is, by accepting her as she is, listening to her without judgement or censure, allowing her to voice her feelings and her opinions. This is not to say that the child-within dictates our lives, but rather that we take her story into account, giving consideration to her point of view. Like all good parents, we need to listen carefully and then make decisions based on what is most appropriate in any given situation without denying our emotional truths. This inner-parent is able to foster a rich and satisfying relationship with the inner-child, comforting her when she needs to be comforted, listening when she needs to be heard, and ensuring that her needs are met.

That part of you who is a parent to this inner-child is your own inner-parent.

Since our inner-child represents our emotions, she will tell us much if we listen carefully. Tired? Confused? Angry? Sad? Happy? Excited? Unsure? Our child will let us know. Why do we feel that way? She will tell us that too. If we listen really attentively, not judging or lecturing her for the way she is feeling, our inner-child will disclose the limiting beliefs that hide beneath the painful feelings and negativity.

Our inner-parent is the internalised voice of our external parents — nurturing us to the same extent and in the same ways they did. But it is also the voice inside us that judges us, threatens us, blames us, criticises us, ignores us, belittles us, demands of us, over-indulges us, neglects us, pushes us, abuses us, nags us, negates us — to the same extent and in the same ways our external parents may have done.

Our inner-parent often endorses the limiting beliefs of our inner-child, judging harshly when the child is hurt or tired or bruised, and nagging the rules of 'how things should be'. When our inner-child is harshly over-ruled by our inner-parent, expected to keep her needs and feelings quiet and hidden, neglected or abused — this is when we feel ragged, worn-out, depressed, guilty, frustrated, confused, anxious.

When our inner-parent and our inner-child are not relaxed and co-operative with each other, we struggle with unresolved internal conflict, painfully aware of its effects on us but often unaware of its roots within ourselves or of how to extricate ourselves.

Our now-self is the outcome of this inner relationship between our inner-child and our inner-parent.

Our now-self is involved constantly in the internal dialogue between these inner aspects. This is the incessant chatter, or self-talk, that goes on inside our heads all day, every day. And when our inner-child and our inner-parent are not considerate of each other, it can sound like this:

Inner-child: 'I'm tired!'
Inner-parent: 'Too bad! We have to keep going!'

Inner-child: 'I hate this job. I'm in a rut.'
Inner-parent: 'You're always complaining. At least we've got a job.'

Inner-parent: 'We really ought to be more reliable.'
Inner-child: 'No-one's going to pin me down.'

Inner-child: 'I'm angry about that.'
Inner-parent: 'It's not worth bothering about. Calm down!'

It is our now-self who may be confused and rendered indecisive by the struggle between our inner-child and our inner-parent; it is our now-self who relaxes when our inner-child and our inner-parent are in agreement; our now-self who is confident and self-fulfilled when our inner-parent and our inner-child co-exist peacefully with mutual respect.

Melissa was not listening to her inner-child. That is, her inner-parent was judging her inner-child, pushing her hard and ignoring her needs and feelings, rather than comforting her and listening carefully to her. If Melissa had allowed her inner-parent to listen to her inner-child she might have heard this child say: 'I feel so tired and I can't go on like this, having to appear cheerful when I don't feel that way, and forced to do things perfectly when I need to rest. Please stop pushing me. Please listen to me'.

How Melissa was now feeling and thinking — the state of her now-self — was a reflection of the relationship between her own inner-parent and inner-child. The relationship was in a state of turmoil and as a result Melissa, here and now, felt anxious, confused and stressed.

Unfortunately many of us have neglected our inner-child for so long that she plays little or no part in our day-to-day living. When the relationship between our inner-parent and inner-child becomes seriously askew; when we judge ourselves; when we give no time or respect to our emotional lives; or conversely, if we allow our emotions to rule us without the moderating influence of reflection and reason: this is when life becomes unsatisfying and difficult — a struggle. It means that we are operating on remote-control, our inner conversations or self-talk being a direct product of the limiting beliefs that we took on in childhood.

It is only when we reconnect with our inner-child — when we learn to parent her lovingly and thoughtfully — that we can begin to recognise and change the limiting beliefs that run us. In Parts Three and Four of the book we will show you how you can start to parent your own inner-child.

It is the inner-child who holds the key to our limiting beliefs.

Before you begin that, however, please realise that for some people, childhood may have involved traumatic events. They may have been severely abandoned or rejected; perhaps their parents were so emotionally injured and fragile themselves that they could not offer the nurture and protection that all children need. In other words, the role models for the developing inner-parent of these children were inadequate or inappropriate.

The messages that these children picked up and the beliefs they subsequently formed about themselves are possibly quite damaging. If you are one of these people, we urge you to seek a professional therapist to help you sort through your early experiences. Trying to parent your own inner-child may be too difficult and painful for you to do on your own, and you may need a trained person to give you the support you need for your first sensitive steps in this arena.

Our many beliefs and how they affect us

We do hold many beliefs that are helpful to us and enhance our experience of life. However, others are unhelpful and limit our experience of life.

For instance, the belief that 'personal problems are a sign of personal deficiency' is likely to be unhelpful and limit us from openly acknowledging difficulties and seeking solutions. On the other hand, the belief that 'personal problems offer a chance to learn and grow' is likely to be more helpful to us and enhance our prospects for finding the best solutions.

Some of our beliefs are helpful in some areas of our life and unhelpful in others. The belief that 'my primary role in life is as a mother' may mean you are happy to be at home and that you do a superb job of parenting. But if this belief excludes you from pursuing other interests, from developing other aspects of your potential and your personality, then it becomes limiting and unhelpful.

We all hold conflicting beliefs. We might hold the belief that 'I must be careful and stay safe, never taking risks', and the belief that 'I must be a successful career person to be accepted', which would be difficult to achieve without some risk-taking. The holding of such opposing beliefs is often the source of inner conflict.

Two of Melissa's beliefs were: 'I'm only acceptable if I am busy' and 'I must always be cheerful so that everyone will like me'. These beliefs conflicted heavily whenever Melissa perceived she was being criticised for not doing enough, or for being lazy. She would feel angry but her belief that she must be cheerful kept her locked into an outward appearance that belied her internal state.

While many of our beliefs may have served us well at one time, they may no longer do so. The belief that 'the way to get attention is to sulk' may have got the desired reaction from Mum — she may have sought us out to talk about what was bothering us, brought us a slice of cake to make us feel better, or promised an outing on the weekend that we would really enjoy. The sulking behaviour made us feel loved and nurtured ultimately, but it is inappropriate behaviour for adult life and will not usually achieve the desired (often subconscious) result. Yet many adults do still sulk, habitually responding to difficulties by withdrawing either physically or emotionally, saying things like 'Just leave me alone. I'm not discussing it!'

We may think that it is our circumstances and the events of our lives that determine our experience of life, but in fact our experience is actually the result of our beliefs. Psychologist Albert Ellis has come up with a model — ABC — that explains just this.

Our beliefs determine how we interpret events.

Let's use an example to illustrate the model. You are feeling unwell and a friend phones to say she will be visiting you that day. You wait in eager anticipation for company all afternoon and your friend does not come. You feel disappointed and let down, and you begin to tell yourself that you shouldn't trust anyone — everyone lets you down eventually so it's best to keep people at a distance. You should have known this would happen, and anyway, nobody thinks that much of you to worry about whether you are sick or not. And so goes the negative self-talk.

What seems to have happened is that the 'Activating event' (A) —

your friend promising to come but then not turning up — has led to the 'Consequence' (C): your feelings of distrust and low self-esteem.

But the 'B' of Ellis's model is what actually intervenes: this is a core Belief that dictates the consequence. In this case there seem to be a couple of beliefs at work. They are something like 'I can't trust anyone' and 'I'm not worth worrying about'.

If you have any doubt about the intervening Belief, keep in mind that the outcome — the Consequence of the Activating event — might have been vastly different. If your core belief went something like 'My friends care deeply for me', then you might react with concern when your friend did not come. Or, if your belief was 'Life is unpredictable', then you might laugh off your friend's not turning up and assume she was caught up in some other activity.

Each time, the Consequence differs purely because the Belief varies.

> A B C
> ACTIVATING EVENT
> BELIEF
> CONSEQUENCE

What we are calling negative self-talk, Ellis calls 'catastrophic thinking'. The above story provides one example of catastrophic thinking, where a friend not arriving leads to self-talk that leads to emotional turmoil — feelings of abandonment and loss of trust, and perhaps even feelings of betrayal.

> Our beliefs determine what we think and feel.

A belief (or irrational assumption, as Ellis would call it) might be something like 'I must please everyone to feel worthwhile'. The catastrophic thinking, the negative self-talk, goes wild if it seems that some person is displeased by something that I do. On the other hand, a belief like 'While I do like to please others, I recognise that it is unrealistic to try to please everyone' is a healthy one and is unlikely to lead to emotional disaster if someone is displeased once in a while.

Allied to Ellis's work is that of Martin Seligman, author of *Learned Optimism*, who maintains that non-biological depression results from the way a person interprets what could be called a negative event. While optimists will view such an event as unpleasant, they will not

With the beliefs that she held — 'I'm acceptable only if I'm busy' and 'It's not safe to relax until *everything* is done' — Melissa usually felt tense, anxious that something might have been overlooked by her and frustrated because everything almost never is done. She was physically exhausted by seven o'clock each evening yet often couldn't sleep because of her inability to switch her brain off from the day's concerns and tomorrow's job lists. The insomnia made her tiredness worse and so it went on until serious health problems were emerging. Resentment ate away at her, especially when she came across people she considered carefree and easygoing. Then her negative thinking or self-talk went along the lines of 'They should realise life is serious' or 'They're so shallow' or 'How can they be so lazy'.

view it as a measure of their worth, whereas pessimists will resort to 'catastrophic thinking', deciding they are hopeless, incompetent, unattractive and worthless.

Seligman's continuing research reveals that optimists enjoy much better health than pessimists and that we can learn to be more optimistic. In other words, we can learn to change our beliefs and so change the way we interpret events.

As we have said before, our beliefs are the single most powerful influence on our intimate day-by-day reality. Since our core beliefs about ourselves and life in general determine our thoughts and feelings, they affect every decision we take, every communication we make, every relationship we are in.

Our beliefs determine how we act and react.
It is easy to see how this is so if I hold the common belief that 'I am of no real value'. I will either sell myself short in myriads of ways, or I may have built a whole army of self-defences around this core belief.

On the surface, I may now be of great value, having spent my life amassing a fortune or doing great charitable works, unaware of my true motivation — to prove myself valuable. I will not, however, feel satisfied and I and everyone else will wonder why. The reason is that I am driven by an underlying limiting belief.

If you feel you are not in the driver's seat in life, you are being driven by your limiting beliefs. This explains, at least in part, why we come across such a wide variety of responses to similar events. One person might react to the promotion of a colleague with excitement and encouraging words, while another might react with resentment and withdrawal of personal friendship. It is not the event itself that directly causes the reaction. Each of these people has a particular belief that dictates their response.

Now, let us suppose that I believe I am unable to hold my own in intellectual conversations. I will become uncomfortable as soon as such a conversation begins and I will be sensitive to others' reactions to my comments, interpreting them as negative. They may laugh in appreciation, and I interpret their response as derision. I will perceive potentially beneficial communications to me as threatening, dismissing any worthwhile thoughts I may have as being not smart enough to utter.

All of these inner reactions will reinforce my belief in my own inadequacy — 'I'll never be a good conversationalist, I'm just not made that way' — and, as well, may trigger my ego-defence ('This is a stupid conversation anyway').

In other words, we see life through our belief systems. Our belief program functions like a gauze screen curving around in front of our ears and our eyes. This screen filters the continuous flow of information coming in to us and selects what will and will not pass into our conscious awareness. We take in only what fits through the filter, what fits our belief system.

We do not see life the way it is, we see it the way we are.

If I have a belief that 'Life is serious', it will not endear fun-loving people to me. I will regard them as shallow and irresponsible, whether they are or not. A belief that 'You should never blow your own trumpet' will prompt inappropriate responses or reactions from me when my small children start insisting I praise their kindergarten paintings, or a friend wants to share her joy in her new-found skills with me. I will see them all as show-offs rather than loved ones attempting to share their joys with me.

Since we feel uncomfortable with situations and people who do not fit through our particular filter, we tend to restrict ourselves to situations and people with whom we do feel comfortable — those who do fit through our filter, our belief program.

All the data coming in to us is examined for any sign of its emphasising our own beliefs. Anything there that does not fit is either overlooked or twisted to fit what our beliefs tell us is the way things really are.

We have all been amazed to hear others interpret a situation in ways we regard as absolutely incorrect, even downright dishonest — as when public figures who have escaped the legal consequences for their corruption earnestly proclaim that 'Justice has been done' when it is obvious that the opposite is the truth. Such people, it seems, often truly believe what they are saying!

Our own special individual filter makes sure that everything else stays out there and only what is 'relevant' to us is let in. What is relevant to us? Those aspects that 'speak' to our beliefs, those aspects that trigger some response in us. The other aspects are rejected by us, although the next person may take them in because that person filters out different things. This process accounts for the way no two of us see an event in exactly the same way. I will notice whatever 'speaks' to my beliefs, and you will notice whatever 'speaks' to your beliefs.

Our very particular individual beliefs actually determine what we are able to see, hear — and do.

Not only do my beliefs cause me to select what I see and hear, and to give particular interpretations to what I see and hear, they also determine my reactions to people and situations. For instance, if I have a belief that 'I must be cautious and never take risks', I interpret a recession as yet another reason for not making that career move. This reinforces my natural tendency to procrastinate and avoid change. The recession exists but it is the way I use that information that allows it to limit me personally.

If I had a contrary belief, 'Change makes life interesting', I might decide to make a career move that gives me change together with security. If I have a belief that 'Life is dull and meaningless without drama going on', I will make a change that is probably disastrous so that I can create more drama. If I believe 'I'm powerless', I will stay in a position that everyone can see is doomed to be axed and become powerless in the face of the recession.

Each one of these responses reinforces the belief that gave rise to it in the first place.

We all know stories of individuals who have burst through a common belief barrier. One famous instance is that of Roger Bannister who, in 1954, achieved the impossible by breaking the four-minute mile. Before long, many other individuals were also running the mile in less than four minutes. Bannister's achievement convinced others that what they had previously thought impossible was now a possible feat.

When we talk about 'our idea of reality' we are saying that each of us has our own reality; we may think that what we are seeing is the ultimate reality, but it is only our interpretation that we are seeing.

Although Melissa cared deeply for Peter, her partner, she found that she was becoming less and less tolerant of some of his ways. It seemed to her that Peter was provoking her by flopping in front of the television to watch sport on Saturday afternoons rather than throwing himself into renovating their terrace house. She was horrified at how lazy he was being and often accused him, in her frustration, of being a 'good-for-nothing'.

Peter, who was finding work very stressful of late, would have liked to talk to Melissa about it but found she never sat still for long enough to listen to him. She was becoming more demanding all the time, he said, and he found himself doing more to avoid her. Here was Peter's belief that 'I can never please people, so why bother' coming into play. Both Melissa and Peter were losing sight of the other as their very individual ideas of reality took over.

Often it is the beliefs of which we are unaware that are the most binding; they restrict our perceptiveness, our ability to relate closely to others, our knowledge, wisdom, expansion and freedom. Our beliefs have become part of who we are, second nature to us, invisible because we take them for granted without questioning them. We do not consider them as beliefs about reality, but as reality itself. We come up with comments like these:

'But life *is* a struggle.'

'But emotions *are* a sign of weakness.'

'But that *is* just the way I am — I can't change.'

These are all beliefs about reality, but they are not in themselves reality. We are usually unaware of most of our limiting beliefs, yet our beliefs program is such that we view our entire field of reality from this position. We proceed through life adding both inner and outer images that reinforce our beliefs, so that we can say things like 'See! I knew it! You just can't trust anyone!' or 'See! I *am* like that!'

> Our beliefs become self-fulfilling prophecies.

The more we live in our limiting-beliefs distorted version of the world, the more convinced we become that this is the true picture of the world and the people in our lives. Just as the screen of our belief systems acts as a filter to incoming experience, it also acts as a haze, a distorting medium, to our outgoing perceptions.

Our beliefs program determines for us whether our behaviour is 'driven' or simply the expression of a conscious choice. Depending on how restrictive our belief system is, we will to a greater or lesser extent be driven. Our experience of life will be more open or more closed, more calm or more turbulent, more happy or less happy.

> Our beliefs determine our experience of life.

As long as our belief system dominates us, the only way we can find happiness is to manipulate the world to fit it. We will need to control others in an attempt to force them to fit our picture of reality, of how 'things should be', thereby causing conflict as others struggle for control of their own lives and to maintain their own version of how 'things should be'. This is the fundamental cause of all forms of violence in our society. Be it child abuse, domestic violence, street crime or theft with assault, all violence is the direct result of what people have grown up to believe about themselves, others and life in general.

A male child growing up with domestic violence can slip easily into the belief that women should do as men say and it's OK to belt them when they don't. Female children growing up with domestic violence often come to believe 'I can't trust anyone — everyone lets me down sooner or later'.

A child growing up with poverty and seeing wealth all around might come to believe that 'Life's unfair, so anything I do to get my needs met is justified'.

Someone who grew up believing in their own helplessness will probably not cope well with a crying, helpless baby.

And on it goes, so that an essential component in reducing violence in society has to be the effective changing of such beliefs at the individual level, for belief programs are passed down from one generation to the next. This explains why people who have been abused often abuse in turn. Changing social conditions (such as poverty) that breed such beliefs is another vital component in repairing our damaged society.

We can hardly blame ourselves, or others, for taking on limiting and sometimes self-destructive and relationship-destructive beliefs, when we realise that these beliefs grew from a child's attempts to

> The unhappier she felt, the harder Melissa tried. Generalising her beliefs to 'People shouldn't be lazy' and 'There's always plenty to be done', she did all she could to get Peter involved in renovation work on the weekend. She tried to maintain a cheerful demeanour, but with deep resentment bubbling underneath, and that only led to more and more frustration as Peter dug in his heels, believing that nothing he did would make a difference anyway. So with their own picture of reality in mind, each tried to control the other and make the other fit into that picture. While each struggled for control, their relationship headed into real difficulties.

survive by adapting to his perceived or real environment. They were the result of a child's attempts to mould himself to maintain parental love, approval and attention.

Uncovering our limiting beliefs

How do we uncover just what our limiting beliefs are? After all, they are often subconscious and it is only the resulting effects that we are aware of, namely our negative thoughts, feelings and outcomes. This is where the clue lies: by examining our negative thoughts and our uncomfortable emotions we can uncover our limiting beliefs.

The keys to our limiting beliefs are our uncomfortable emotions and our negative thoughts.

Therefore the first step is to acknowledge and accept our uncomfortable emotions and our negative thoughts because they are the keys that can unlock our most sought-after answers.

This does not mean that they need engulf us or direct our actions. In the workbook sections of this book, you will learn how to use them creatively and effectively to your benefit.

As you engage in the conscious process of allowing your negative thoughts and uncomfortable emotions to lead you to awareness of your limiting beliefs, you will be able to change those beliefs to enhancing beliefs of your own choosing, using the specific skills you will learn here. You will notice your uncomfortable feelings falling away, as their source — your beliefs — is dismantled.

Our case studies will give more detailed examples of this process but let us consider one simple example. Jocelyn is a young woman who decided to tackle the uncomfortable feelings that made themselves felt during certain interactions with a workmate. Using some of the ideas in our workbook section she focussed carefully on those feelings instead of trying to avoid them by keeping herself constantly busy. As she allowed herself — her inner-child — to express herself freely and fully around her discomfort and negativity rather than deflecting it onto her workmate, and as she listened carefully and openly to this part of herself, she soon became aware that underneath her feelings of resentment and jealousy lay a real competitiveness. Further open listening made it obvious that the belief underlying these feelings was 'I have to be better than anyone else, otherwise I am no good at all'.

Uncovering this belief was a source of great amusement to Jocelyn, and she could see why she had taken it on, considering the sorts of messages she picked up during her formative years.

Using the processes outlined in Part Four of our book, she was able to 'reprogram' — to change this belief into one that worked for her rather than against her, resulting in more positive feelings that increased self-esteem. It was only then that the uncomfortable feelings which first alerted her to look within herself abated and she was able to respond differently — more constructively and more appropriately — to her workmate.

> It is by accepting and listening to our negative thoughts and emotions that we free ourselves from them.

The problem with positive thinking

You might have many preconceptions and habits (beliefs) about dealing with negative thinking. The most common belief is that it is something to be avoided and that we should steer our minds onto positive thinking. Of course, the harder we try to do this, the more we struggle within ourselves.

Sometimes we have been told to think positively, to smile and be cheerful no matter what is going on around us. Schools of 'positive thinking' were an early development and were on the right track. But any attempt to force positive thoughts upon yourself when you have not uncovered and dealt with the specific limiting beliefs causing the negative thinking often does more harm than good. You have probably had the experience of 'positive thinking' lasting for a while only to dissipate and you're back where you started, but worse off because now you believe you have failed, and you may well feel guilty or depressed or demoralised.

We may succeed for a time, but inevitably the negative thoughts resurface and so do the uncomfortable feelings. This is because the limiting beliefs causing the negative thinking are more deeply and more strongly held than this. Put in self-parenting terms, our inner-child, who is our emotional and historical selves and who holds our limiting beliefs, will not be dismissed or denied by a glib message from our inner-parent, who is our rational selves.

> **With positive thinking we are merely trying to place a band-aid over the symptom (our negative thoughts) rather than dealing with the cause — our limiting beliefs.**

Some myths about negative emotions

We have been taught to flee from our negative emotions, to undertake all kinds of manoeuvres to avoid them, to distract ourselves from them in endless ways, and even to deny their very existence. This seems a logical message, since our negative emotions are painful. Some schools of personal growth teach us to realise that it is our negative thinking that causes our negative emotions and the answer is therefore to change our negative thinking to positive thinking, using techniques of varying levels of sophistication.

You will have had the experience of 'bottling up' emotions that you did not want to know about or did not feel free to express. But what often happens? Sooner or later you dissolve into tears, or succumb to anxiety, or explode, or anger leaks out of you like poison in nasty little sideswipes of sarcasm or passive aggression such as the silent or superior treatment.

This happens because 'emotion' is 'energy-in-motion'. The word comes from the Latin *ex movere* which means 'to move outwards'. If we block the energy it stays locked inside us, trying to move out. Nature has provided us with spontaneous release mechanisms, for we naturally and spontaneously *make* love, *jump* for joy, *cry* in sorrow, *tremble* with fear and *blush* with embarrassment. This understanding of emotions as energy is discussed further in this book.

Negative emotions cannot be suppressed or denied forever.

For now our point is that, put in self-parenting terms, this inevitable expression of negative emotion means that our inner-child, who is our emotional/energy selves, will not be suppressed or held in check forever by prohibitive messages from our inner-parent, who is our rational selves. Many of us keep the lid on our uncomfortable feelings for years, but this requires enormous effort — both mental and physical. We chronically tense our bodies to restrict the natural flow of emotional energy. This effort uses up stores of our mental and physical energy that we could be using for more creative purposes. Sooner or later this effort catches up with us — perhaps in a mid-life crisis, physical collapse, or fatigue and illness — as a result of our misguided struggle.

So stop struggling!

Melissa truly believed that any negative emotion was not to be expressed. She believed she must always have a happy, cheerful attitude, and that she should avoid either acknowledging within herself or expressing outwardly anything that could possibly be interpreted as negative. Even when her colleagues made mistakes or did not complete things as she would have liked, she gritted her teeth, smiled, and went about trying to improve things. Much of her physical tension was the result of the effort of trying to suppress her increasingly distressing emotions.

The productive use of negative thoughts and emotions

It is as false to deny our negative thoughts and emotions as it is to deny the existence of wind and snow. And just because wind and snow exist, there is no reason for us to live perpetually exposed to them. The same is true of our negative thoughts and uncomfortable emotions. We can either try to keep them inside, punishing ourselves

We have a choice about how to use our negative thoughts and emotions.

and others with them, or we can succumb to them and lose ourselves in negative overwhelm, or we can acknowledge them and learn from them so that we can change the beliefs causing them.

It is your choice — choose wisely!

The two keys to your inner self, to greater awareness and thereby to more conscious control over the outcomes in your life, are:

Uncomfortable emotions.

Negative thoughts.

These are the keys in your possession that, if used appropriately, can unlock your full potential as a human being. They are the clues that, if followed instead of suppressed or denied or wallowed in, can reveal to you what your self-limiting beliefs are.

Melissa wanted help. She was more than happy to begin uncovering her beliefs and clarifying them. She did this by accepting rather than denying all the negative thoughts and feelings that were causing her so much distress. By paying attention to the frustration she felt — the anxiety, the resentment — and listening to her own negative thoughts, she started to be aware of the limiting beliefs that lay beneath those thoughts and feelings. In other words, Melissa was learning the art of good self-parenting. She was starting to converse with her inner-child, listening well to how she honestly felt. In this way, Melissa could start to uncover her limiting beliefs.

Beliefs about anger

Of course it is the emotion of anger that causes the most concern. We may have been led to believe anger itself is dangerous. It is not, but what we do in response to that emotion may or may not be dangerous.

Anger charges part of the nervous system for our instinctive 'fight or flight' mechanism on perceived attack. However, the evolution of the human mind takes us beyond instinctive reaction to a more considered response. Yet we must still find appropriate ways to release the energy of our anger. Only when we have dealt with its energy rush can we resolve it and learn from it about the beliefs that caused it.

There are basically three belief systems about anger, each accompanied by a particular personality style.

If you are an anger suppressor you may think, 'I never/seldom feel angry'. Unless you have reached a state of life where you are totally fulfilled and happy, what you are really saying is: 'I never allow myself to feel my anger. I have learnt to totally/generally disconnect from it because I have beliefs that cause me to deny it'.

Some of us have easier access to our anger than others. Indeed many of us spread our anger about quite liberally in explosive attacks or acid remarks. We are the anger-expressors. Anger-dumping is our speciality. Those of us who do this usually hold beliefs such as 'Others cause my anger' or 'Others ought to do this / be like that' or 'Others ought to look after me'.

The truth is, others do what they do and different people will react in different ways. If I react with anger, it is my anger. If I want to change the situation or the way the other person is acting, attacking doesn't usually help. If I want to keep my anger and feel self-righteous, I can go on blaming the person who provoked it. But if I want to be rid of it I simply have to own it as mine before I can begin to do anything constructive about the situation or person causing it.

Only very occasionally is our anger 'clean' — that is, really caused by a particular event. Mostly the event that triggered it did just that — it triggered an inner store of anger that we carry around with us just below the surface all the time. We are seldom angry at what we think we are angry at.

If we are neither an anger-suppressor nor an anger-expressor, then perhaps we drip our anger on others in simmering resentment. We are the resentors. We withdraw to punish, we arch our eyebrows, we huff our superiority, sulk and pout, moan and groan, change the subject, cry tears of reproach, manipulate, to get even. We hold beliefs such as 'Others should be like this' or 'You should do this' or 'You should respond to me this way' and 'Nice people don't show anger so I won't'. In other words, we carry both sets of beliefs, those of both the expressors and the suppressors.

Anger is, like all emotions, energy. We use many expressions that confirm that emotions are energy-in-motion. We talk of 'butterflies in our stomach', 'our heart leaping into our mouths', we say he 'blew his top', we have 'a lump in the throat'. Although the human body is designed to accept the free flow of the energy of an emotion, our social conditioning often makes this unacceptable. From an early age we learn to block the energy flow. Men learn not to 'burst into tears', children learn to 'contain' their enthusiasm and most of us learnt to 'keep the lid on' our anger, all in the name of 'maturity'.

But the energy has to go somewhere. If blocked it becomes locked up in muscle tension, when its natural way would be to flow out of us. So it is healthy to develop appropriate strategies for diverting the physical energy of our anger away from any personal target. Sport seems to have become an institutionalised way of releasing anger in our society. But it is more effective to consciously expend anger-energy by finding a place where we can be on our own, focussing on whatever it is that is triggering our anger, and doing something energetic, voicing our angry thoughts while we do so. We can go for a jog, belt a punching bag, slam into the bed with the flat of a racquet or our fists, throw a tantrum on the bed, or just plain yell and shout.

If all of this sounds too foreign to you, you are no doubt an anger-suppressor or a resentor, and the process would be invaluable for you. At least begin by picking a time and place where you will not be overheard and allowing yourself to 'sound off' to yourself.

Do whatever releases the energy. None of this leads to insanity! In fact, after appropriately releasing the energy of anger, we can think more clearly and calmly about the problem and what best to do about it, and make any necessary communications more 'cleanly'.

What is decidedly unhelpful to ourselves or to our relationships is to dump the energy onto another person, either directly in an angry outburst, or indirectly in smears of resentment. It is much better to handle the energy first, then calmly and clearly communicate what you are angry about.

The very best thing to do with our anger, as with any other negative emotion, is to uncover the limiting belief causing it. When we change that belief we no longer respond with anger or with any other uncomfortable emotion. We are then free — no longer at the mercy of others or of external situations. We can then actually perceive the person or situation clearly and so make the most appropriate decisions and take the most appropriate actions.

It didn't take Melissa long to acknowledge that she harboured great resentment (which was in fact anger), which she expressed in the typical resentor mode: by withdrawing, by sulking, by rolling her eyes and shaking her head, by sarcastic words spread with honey. Her belief that she should be cheerful at all times had ensured that she never expressed her anger openly.

Once she was aware of the origins of her anger — at being denied a carefree childhood, at her belief that she must always try so hard to please others, at her belief that she must keep running at breakneck speed to get everything done as perfectly as possible — she could begin to express it physically. In the privacy of her bedroom, she pounded her bed with great force while loudly voicing her rage at this programming. 'Unburdened' and 'exhilarated' was how she described feeling afterwards. Melissa's change process was now well under way. She had begun to reclaim her own power over her painful beliefs and to develop an understanding of the importance of truthfully communicating her feelings.

Our beliefs and our needs

Our uncomfortable emotions and negative thoughts reveal something else as well as our limiting beliefs. They can be used to clarify our unmet needs.

As human beings we have certain needs beyond those necessary for survival. We have needs for love, for security, for acknowledgment, for understanding. We all share the same needs but the extent to which they are important to us varies from person to person. Emotional security is a much more urgent need for some people than it is for others. Acknowledgment may be more important to me than it is to you. It depends on the extent to which these needs were or were not met in childhood.

As adults, our needs are often not met for a variety of reasons, but most often it is because we have beliefs that prevent our getting those needs met. A person who needs acknowledgment may have a strong belief that 'To call attention to oneself is not OK' and that 'One should not blow one's own trumpet'. This person will not be open about their accomplishments, may defer when asked about them but, inside, needs someone to turn up and recognise their worth. Their need, then, may go mostly unmet. Indeed, we may know of women whose need for a stable family life is thwarted by a belief that 'Men can't be trusted', or of men whose need for intimacy is undermined by the belief that 'Displays of emotion are only for women and are a sign of immaturity in men'.

Many of us go through life hoping that one day someone or something — the right job, idea, place — will turn up and all will be well. This is the prevalent 'The grass is greener on the other side of the hill' syndrome. So if this relationship isn't working out, we try another, without stopping to look within ourselves first. Most of us don't stop to clarify our true needs so that we can find or recognise the right person or opportunity when they do turn up.

How many of us actually make a list of what we want in a life partner? Sounds strange? Only because hardly anyone does it. And yet, it seems an odd thing not to do given that this is one of the most important choices we make in our entire lives.

Our favourite real-life story about how ignorant we all can be when it comes to our own needs is that of Cathy. Cathy was a very intelligent woman, an architect, who undertook this needs-clarifying exercise after two disastrous marriages.

She discovered that she had a belief, held by many of us, that 'I can never get my emotional needs met'. As she worked to change this belief she saw that the men she had chosen (because, after all, no-one had made her choose them) had only two or three of the twenty-two characteristics she needed for a committed, conscious, intimate relationship. That is far more strange, surely!

And yet we settle down with someone because we have fallen in love, not realising that this very state has little to do with loving someone, which can be done only when we know someone well enough.

A year and a half later she took a look at her list. She was actually stunned to realise that this was a precise description of a man she had met six months ago and come to know very well, but she had not considered him romantically because he did not fit her picture of a life partner. He was very quiet, not at all the urbane man-about-town she had always gone for in the past.

We like this story not just because Cathy now lives happily with her quiet prince but also because it demonstrates so clearly some facts about needs.

Many of us hold beliefs that actively prevent us from getting our most basic needs met.

Our needs are our responsibility and no-one else's. To accept this responsibility means to be clear about what they are and take appropriate action to get them met.

To do this does not mean we are self-centred but rather that we are responsible. Taking responsibility for our basic needs does not mean pandering to our every whim and fancy. As we become more satisfied with life, we become more loving, open and creative and so contribute to the wellbeing and happiness of others.

Being clear makes it possible to see clearly.

So, uncomfortable emotions and negative thoughts can reveal not only what our self-limiting beliefs are, but also exactly what our unmet needs are.

When considering her limiting beliefs, it was clear to Melissa that her unmet needs were:

To be accepted for who she is, not for what she does.

To feel safe to relax.

To feel safe to express her feelings openly.

Acknowledging that these needs were her responsibility led Melissa to see that it was she who had to give herself the unconditional acceptance her inner-child craved. She also saw that this would make it safe for her to relax and express her feelings.

These are fundamental human needs that her beliefs program actively prevented her from ever having met. She had been trying to find contentment and fulfilment the way we all do at first — by striving harder to do more of the same and by insisting that those close to us join in. After all, we think, these are the people who are meant to make us happy, so they should join us in our efforts to be happy. So Melissa worked harder, relaxed less and denied her feelings more, all the while feeling frustrated and alone because her partner could not join her in what was essentially *her* struggle.

Core beliefs and branch beliefs

Our beliefs program is like a tree. It has a trunk from which have grown branches. Someone from an emotionally deprived childhood might easily form all kinds of beliefs such as 'Others should look after me' and 'Life is scary' and 'No matter what I do I never get attention'. These could all be branches of a core belief that 'I am powerless to have my needs met'.

If this person were to change this core belief, then they would discover that the branch limiting beliefs would fall away too. It is as though we cut down the trunk and the whole tree falls with it. It is therefore more productive to work on core beliefs than on branch beliefs. Indeed, if you begin working on a branch belief you will soon discover that there is another belief hidden beneath it, supporting it, feeding it, and that you must do your change work on that core belief in order to permanently stop the branch from re-growing. However, if you begin chopping away at a branch, you will more easily see the trunk and be able to move in on it.

Melissa considered her beliefs:

People shouldn't be lazy.

There's always plenty to be done.

Life is serious.

It's not safe to relax until everything is done.

I must always be cheerful to be liked.

And saw that they were all branches of a core belief: 'If I do not please others and do everything perfectly I am not acceptable *to myself*'.

The belief she needed to put in place to topple the whole program was 'I accept myself just as I am'. Then she would be able to express her feelings without self-judgement, to honour her need to have more fun, to relax when she needed and so also to respect other people's need to relax.

As these new beliefs took hold she began to think and feel differently, and consequently she began to see things differently and to behave differently too.

She now saw Peter's insistence on a balance between rest and work as healthier for both herself and their relationship. She took the time to listen to him when he needed to confide his problems. She began to value spending quality time together and watched it strengthening their relationship. With this change in Melissa, Peter was happy to pour energy into the renovations and Melissa reported, laughing at her own irony, 'Things are coming along like a house, not on fire, but being built'.

Changing our limiting beliefs

In Part Four we give you the tools for changing your limiting beliefs. The main thing to understand about this change process is that it simply is not possible to affect permanent inner change in your head alone, for your beliefs are held as much in your emotions (that is, by your inner-child), in your energy system (emotions are energy, as we have seen), and in your body itself, as they are in your head. It is no use trying to permanently change your limiting beliefs as a purely intellectual exercise.

Permanent change cannot be effected at the intellectual level alone.

Our case studies in Part Two will demonstrate this to you and in Part Four we give you a way to effect change taking all this into account.

We took on most of our limiting beliefs originally as a way of adapting to our childhood environment, and we did this because we considered these beliefs to be the very best way to make sense of, and indeed survive in, our environment. So our inner-child may take a little convincing that any particular belief is no longer necessary for survival. Our self-parenting exercises will help you with this aspect.

Also, we can be attached to a particular belief because there is often a pay-off for holding onto the belief. In a self-destructive way, we do derive a 'benefit' from it. For example, if I hold a belief that 'Life happens to me and I am powerless' then I get to be 'not responsible' for whatever happens to me. If I hold a belief that 'I have to get everything right' and I have spent my life ensuring that I usually do, then I probably get to feel superior to most other people because they appear to 'get things wrong' a lot of the time.

Another reason for not wanting to let go of a limiting belief is that our child-within may not feel it is safe to let go of that belief. If again I hold the belief that 'I am powerless' then I may have built up an armoury of branch beliefs about power, such as 'Power is dangerous' 'Powerful people are not good people'. Indeed, when I was a child, such may have been my very experience of 'power', or what I then perceived to be 'power'.

It is quite common for the child-within to be afraid to let go of the old belief, to feel that it is not safe to do so. After all, she has clung to it for this long for the very good reason that it made sense of things once, however painfully.

> Even though our limiting beliefs cause us pain and struggle, we are often deeply attached to them.

As human beings our inherent potential is boundless and therefore the process of personal growth is endless — we can go on and on expanding beyond limits, rather like a set of Russian dolls that emerge each from within the other, expanding to fill each new space available to us.

As we break free from our currently most pressing limiting beliefs we experience expansion and joy. And on we go until we encounter our next set of barriers, from which we can use the same knowledge and techniques to break free.

A person with a core belief of 'I don't matter much' would break out of this first barrier to the next which might be 'It's not safe to take risks', to the next which might be 'I should not blow my own trumpet', to the next which might be 'Life was not meant to be fun', and so on. Instead of holding these crippling and pain-inducing beliefs, this person would now believe: 'I matter! And it's safe to take risks! What's more, I'm creative and it's OK to let the world know. And life is fun!'

The person would now feel much freer, happier and more productive, as you can be too. You can use the processes and knowledge in this book over and over because when you keep outgrowing limiting beliefs, life simply keeps getting better and better.

Freeing ourselves from our limiting beliefs is a life-long process. The first barrier, our first limiting belief, is the most restrictive and the most painful and once we are free of it the issues involved in each subsequently encountered limiting belief are usually less dire in their consequences. At any moment when you are experiencing painful or merely uncomfortable feelings, you have two choices — go ahead and argue for your limitations and keep your pain, or clarify and change the limiting belief that is causing your pain and grow out of it.

Blaming others for the way you feel and blaming circumstances for your unwanted outcomes will keep you locked into negativity and struggle.

The answers lie in stepping out of blame altogether and looking for your own blameless, limiting beliefs. This will enable you to see things clearly and so take the very best actions to resolve whatever difficulties you face. The choice is always yours and it is a choice you face every time you feel a negative emotion or think a negative thought.

Wherever you place blame, there also you place your power.

Once you have worked through Part Three to clarify your limiting beliefs, you will not have to repeat all of this work again. Whenever you experience strong negative thoughts or emotions, you can simply listen to the voice of your inner-child and let her freely tell you all about that negativity. If you do this you will quickly hear the limiting belief that is causing your discomfort and be able to move straight into changing it.

The main point to remember about uncomfortable emotions and negative thinking is never to judge, deny or repress them. For most of us that's easier said than done, so our workbook section contains a variety of exercises designed to facilitate this vital inner change.

Your outcomes in life
are primarily the result of
your decisions, actions, re-actions and
communications ...

Which are the result of
your thoughts and feelings ...

Which are the result of
your beliefs and your needs.

Your unwanted outcomes in life
are primarily the result of the same dynamics.

PART TWO
Beliefs in Action

Introduction

Our beliefs programs are uniquely ours, because no-one had exactly the same childhood circumstances as we did, not even our siblings. The case studies here are examples only of how beliefs are formed, their effects on our lives, and how they might be changed. You may have in you some of Allan's characteristics, a variation on Emma's theme, or something akin to Melissa's programming. You may recognise that you have Kerry's particular beliefs program, but that you did not have the same childhood history out of which her beliefs grew.

You are indeed unique, as are we all. For this reason, we suggest you do not attempt to set about changing your own beliefs until you have personally done the beliefs-clarifying exercises in Part Three of this book. You are more likely to be successful if you first experience direct contact with the child within you who formed the beliefs, for it is this experiential contact that is the basis of your change work. Furthermore, the change work is a total program.

In our case studies we have highlighted various aspects of that total program that were especially important to individuals. However, this doesn't imply that if you identify with a particular person's beliefs you can change yours by doing only the parts of the change program we have mentioned in relation to that particular person.

You are you — different, unique.

The workbook section, which is the second half of this book, will enable you to clarify your own unique programming and teach you the skills and techniques required to change it. The aim of the case studies is to give you a feel for how beliefs operate in our lives, especially how our limiting beliefs cause us to struggle and suffer, as well as an understanding of the basic principles involved in changing them.

Allan
'I have to get it right or I'm a failure'

It was when Allan exploded at work one day that he realised things were not right for him. As the head of a team, he was well liked and respected by his colleagues. Even though Allan was softly spoken and approachable, his co-workers recognised that he was frequently very tense and they often suggested various ways in which he could learn to relax more.

'I can hardly believe the way I lost my temper,' he said. 'Even when people at work aren't doing their best I try to control myself although I'd like to tell them off sometimes, and I do let them know when it's just not up to scratch. How can they live with themselves when they turn out a report that's sub-standard, I ask myself. This time, though, I really snapped. I don't know why, except that I could feel this tension building and building in me.'

Allan was even less patient with himself than he was with his workmates. He found it very difficult to relax and he put enormous energy into ensuring that every last detail of all he did was taken care of, from planning a family outing to clearing his desk to keeping everything in the right place.

His family bore the brunt of his perfectionism. His lack of spontaneity, his need to pre-plan everything and to mull over even the smallest decision for long periods of time drove them to distraction. His wife commented: 'I try to accept that it's just the way he is, but I feel so frustrated by it all. He is a deeply caring husband and father, very reliable and capable, but he believes strongly that if a thing's worth doing, it's worth doing well. There's nothing wrong with that, but for Allan it means that he puts time and energy into things that just don't warrant that sort of attention. I often feel that family life is on hold while Allan works on getting all the tiny details perfect.'

Although Allan was a loving father, he did make demands on his children to get everything right. While his daughter took it in her stride, avoiding confrontation by quietly doing her best, his fourteen-year-old son had obviously rebelled, adopting a 'see-if-I-care' attitude to his schoolwork and everything else besides. Allan regarded his son as lazy and sloppy, while his wife saw him as a normal fourteen-year-old boy. As a result, there was constant tension in the house. Allan was seeing his son through the filter of his perfectionist belief.

We see life — including others — the way we are.

It was the work episode that finally drove Allan to seek help, although he was reluctant. 'I've been feeling tense for such a long time, and I could say it's just that I need a holiday, but I've just had one. I'm curious about how I could learn to relax,' he said.

Learning relaxation techniques was certainly helpful to Allan, but he needed more: uncovering the beliefs that were keeping him locked into a drive for perfection was actually the key to a more relaxed life for him.

Allan had been the older of two children and he had always felt that his sister was favoured over him. This is a frequent impression amongst eldest children who had their parents to themselves for a time, only to have to make way abruptly for the new arrival. Allan's mother knew she would only have two children so both she and Allan's father had been overjoyed to have a girl the second time and proceeded to treat her as their 'precious princess'.

In this situation Allan struggled to regain primacy in his parents' hearts, only to feel it always eluded him. The result was the belief 'No matter how hard I try, it's never good enough'. On top of this, Allan's parents were both very particular about things being done just so and he took on the additional belief 'I have to get it right or else I am a failure'. The two beliefs fed each other.

Being human, Allan did make mistakes occasionally, and he didn't always meet his own high standards. The result, of course, was deep frustration and an intolerance of others' efforts.

Using the self-parenting methods we present in Part Three, Allan discovered inside himself an exhausted, frazzled little boy, longing for unconditional approval. He had learnt early in his life that to be accepted and approved of he had to get things exactly right. Whether this was the overt message in his home is not the point. Rather, it was what Allan programmed from what he absorbed from his environment at the time. This belief was central to his behaviour for all of his life.

He used self-parenting to listen to that part of himself that was the exhausted little boy, and was profoundly moved by the guided visualisation in which he returned to his childhood home and 'rescued' his inner-child from the demands placed on him (Part Three, page 95). He recognised these demands in his own current self-talk: 'You can do better than that', 'Don't be so slack', 'Are you sure it's all A1?', 'Get your act together', 'Near enough is not good enough', 'Don't just sit here!', 'There's too much to be done to sit around reading'.

Our beliefs determine what we think and feel.

He solemnly undertook to protect this child part of him from these inner demands by learning to stop placing them on him himself. He enlisted his wife by asking her to constantly remind him, when he was overdoing things, that 'It's safe to relax when you need to'. This affirmative message took the place of her former ineffective pleas, such as 'Oh, give it a break!'

Allan had to acknowledge that by keeping his limiting belief and always being the 'perfect' one, he gained the pay-off of feeling self-righteous. So his self-parenting also involved convincing his inner-child, who liked this feeling, that he would actually feel much better if they changed the offending belief.

In fact, in accepting that forgetting things or making mistakes is not a reflection on one's personal worth and does not mean one is a failure, Allan saw that his own worth is intrinsic and not dependent on how well he does anything. Convincing himself — his inner-child — of this allowed him to relax, accept himself unconditionally, and be more tolerant of others when they, too, made mistakes.

Allan was gradually able to choose whether to do something perfectly or to accept that in some particular case or other it really was not important. His professional work was completed to his established high standards, but it no longer mattered if things were not put away for a while, or if something was forgotten on a family outing.

Realising how his core beliefs were affecting his children, he set about easing up on them both. 'I could never see what I was doing before,' he said. 'It isn't that I don't think it's important to do things well any more, but now I see how obsessed I was with that idea. I want to encourage the kids to aim to do the best they can, rather than to aim for perfection.'

Within the month, the school counsellor called the family to let them know that she felt their son no longer needed to see her. He had settled down at school, she told them, and his teachers were noticing that he was taking more interest in his work. When Allan asked his son whether seeing the counsellor had helped him change his attitude, his son replied immediately: 'No, Dad. It's you. You've got off my back.' Allan's experience with his son highlights the fact that when children are playing up, the answer is usually found when the parents change something they are doing. Allan's moving away from his perfectionist beliefs program was already showing results.

Many people in Western society are driven by a 'perfectionist' beliefs program. This program can be one of the major causes of ill health and poor-quality relationships. To change it requires an acceptance of self divorced from what one does and to accept oneself for who one is. This is one of the basic principles of any personal change work, and certainly must be the fundamental attitude brought to any attempt to change one's beliefs. This shift also enables us to be more accepting and less judgemental of others.

We are talking about unconditional self-acceptance as a fundamental component of working on one's beliefs. Acceptance does not mean that I do not want to change parts of myself, or that I agree with my limiting beliefs, or want to keep my frustration or anxiety or sadness. It does mean that I understand how I came to be the way that I am, through my childhood attempts to adjust to my surroundings, and to keep the all-important attention, love and approval from my parents. It does mean that I understand and love that child within me who struggled then and has struggled so hard since then (in whatever ways, productive and self-destructive) to be noticed, approved of and loved. Above all, it means that I learn to listen to all parts of myself with unconditional acceptance.

Self-acceptance is a vital basis for all personal change work.

This is also the key to stepping out of the 'perfection' beliefs program. For Allan and many like him, the first major step into self-acceptance came with his first encounter with his inner-child. Imagining 'rescuing' this child and promising to care for his unmet needs for time and relaxation, filled him with a gentle tenderness towards himself. He reinforced this change by regular self-parenting, and the use of an affirmation specifically designed to change his particular beliefs.

Emma
'All I have to do is be bright and fun to be around'

Emma's story is quite different from Allan's, although she also sought help because of work-related problems.

Emma was instantly likeable: bright, talkative, full of great ideas and endless enthusiasm. She had lots of friends and at twenty-five her life was a whirl of activity. But Emma was feeling the pressure at work. 'It's all too demanding,' she said, 'and my boss expects too much of me. I can never get through the amount of work she expects me to do in a day, and it's not that I'm slow. She says I'm too disorganised or I'd be able to get it all done in time.'

At work her desk was chaotic, as was her filing cabinet. She enjoyed great popularity, but only with those whom her lack of structure and order did not affect greatly. Her boss liked Emma and considered her bright and competent but she found her unable to focus on a task for any length of time.

Emma was currently working in her third position in four years. Twice before she had found herself in an 'overly-demanding' work situation and had found a new job each time. Now she was in the same position and anxious about taking the same way out.

'There are real opportunities there if I can stick it out,' she said. 'This is the third time things have come to this point and friends have suggested that perhaps I am caught in some sort of pattern, so I've decided to look into it and change myself if that's what it takes.'

What Emma was considering was the possibility that her own behaviour was behind her dissatisfaction at her workplace. She tried some of the beliefs-clarifying exercises in Part Three and became aware of how much of an effect her over-indulgent mother had had on her. She had idolised Emma, a long-wanted child to whom she could rarely say 'No!', so Emma rarely had limits placed on her.

She was outgoing and fun-loving — characteristics her mother was proud of in her — and she was not expected to take responsibility for the consequences of her behaviour. Her mother always did all the tidying and cleaning after Emma had entertained her numerous friends at home. In short, Emma was a 'spoilt' child.

Emma began asking the same friends who had tactfully suggested she look at the patterns in her life, whether her behaviour caused problems for them. Her closest friend and flatmate Jane laughed and said, 'Problems? Honey, you're one problem after the next, but you're such fun you get away with it.' 'OK,' said Emma.'Out with it, the full story — from your side, please!'

'Well, here goes. You, my dear friend, are the most unreliable person I've ever known. We all joke that "There's one thing you can rely on about Emma, and that is that she's reliably unreliable". You get all these fantastic ideas, but you don't think them through before you involve others. For instance, last week you decided you were going to go for a jog each night before dinner and you asked if I minded if we had dinner half-an-hour later in future. I rearranged my evening plans to suit. But you haven't been out jogging once! On Saturday you raced out the door, calling "I'll be back in an hour". So I waited because the night before we'd agreed to go to the beach on Saturday. But you didn't come back for four hours.

'You cause such chaos and every time you say, "Sorry! I forgot!" as though that is a good excuse. I know you mean what you say at the time you say you'll do something, but you seem to let every slightest thing blow you off course. You're like a leaf in the wind. You don't seem to even know that that's not the way most adults behave — that it's important to not only mean what you say, but to see it through.

'This is what causes me to "go off the deep end", as you put it, every now and then. I'm pretty easygoing, but each time you do something like this, the anger inside me builds up until the final straw, and I explode. Then you tell me to calm down and not to get so upset over such a little thing, and when I remind you of all the "little things" recently, you think I'm being petty. So I've never been able to make you see. We've been living together for six months now, and I have to tell you I'm seriously considering not renewing the lease with you. As long as we don't live together, we get along much better. Then we can just go out and have fun times like we used to.'

Emma realised that what Jane had said tallied with what her boss was saying and with her discovery that her inner-child was running her personality. The belief 'All I have to do to win approval and attention is be bright and fun to be around' had led to so much chaos in her life because it did not require any structure or order. In effect, it gave total power to her inner-child, allowing her total spontaneity and freedom to express herself without the gentle but firm reining in that is required for effective functioning in the world.

Having clarified her belief, Emma set about righting the imbalance

Our now-self is the result of the relationship between our inner-child and our inner-parent.

in her nature. When she had the 'conversations' with her inner-child that are outlined in Parts Three and Four, she had to spend time convincing her inner-child that she would actually be happier if she accepted some self-imposed boundaries or 'rules'. Of course, Emma's pay-off in keeping her limiting belief was that she was able to stay irresponsible and be 'free' as she saw it.

But her recognition of the costs of keeping the belief — lack of fulfilment in her work, superficial relationships with friends, and ultimately alienation from friends — now enabled her to successfully convince herself (that is, her emotional self) that the pay-off was a poor deal. She learnt to meditate to still the whirl of chatter and ideas in her mind, and she designed for herself an affirmation: 'For my own greater fulfilment, I now choose to be organised and reliable'.

Shortly afterwards she undertook a formal course in time management which proved very helpful. 'A lot of it was just good old commonsense,' she said, 'but I know that if I had done that course before I had come to grips with that basic belief of mine and done some work on changing it, it would have been a waste of time for me because I would not have been disciplined enough to utilise the suggestions they gave.'

Emma continues to be a bright, fun-loving person who attracts people to her. The difference these days is that she has a sense of direction and realises that it is through her own efforts at self-discipline that work will get done and friendships will be nurtured, resulting in her feeling more fulfilled all round.

Gai and Carol
'My feelings are not important'

Gai and Carol were two women who shared the sense of 'Is this all there is? I should be happy, but something is missing and I don't know what it is.' Both women expressed the desire to feel more alive, to improve their relationships with their husbands, whom they saw as remote and preoccupied, to deal with their sense of boredom and to have more energy.

Gai had been married for twenty-three years to a successful businessman, had two children at university, financial affluence, a circle of friends and interests of her own.

Carol had been married for almost as long and was the financial adviser to a large company. She saw herself as emerging from a difficult time. Some months before, her husband had revealed that he had a brief affair with a woman at work. Priding herself on her maturity and her ability to handle difficulties, Carol decided to rise above all this, understanding that mid-life ructions do happen.

'I've read a lot of books about relationships and personal development,' she said, 'and I decided that I could be strong and that way the family would remain intact. It wasn't as if the affair went on and on. It lasted a short time, and I was able to hold myself together during that time and afterwards, too. I'm glad I did, because it's all over now and life is going on as usual.'

Apart from the outward appearance of having everything under control and their desire to 'feel more alive', Gai and Carol had something else in common: they gave earnest and caring advice, even when it wasn't asked for. Both believed that it is important to 'realise that others have problems too', that one 'should make the most of things', that you 'can't let yourself be dragged down by life's difficulties' and so on.

While the motivation behind such advice-giving might be care and concern, the problem is that the person at the other end of the advice may have a belief that makes it damaging to them. A person whose core belief runs something like 'I am powerless to change anything. Nothing I do ever makes any difference' may come away feeling more inadequate than ever after being advised to 'pull themselves together' or 'just get on with it'.

The point is that others might well follow the advice often suggested by rescuers like Gai and Carol, if they could. Their problem is precisely that they are unable to, so such 'helpful' suggestions merely rub salt in their wounds and reinforce their limiting self-esteem beliefs which are the core of their problem.

As Gai and Carol listened to their self-talk in the beliefs clarification exercises in Part Three, they could hear how consistently they rationalised themselves out of their emotions with thoughts like 'That's no reason to get upset', 'Stop over-reacting', 'Good grief, how childish!', 'Pull yourself together'. Listening to such self-talk enabled them to pinpoint their core beliefs and their unmet needs.

Gai's parents had been deeply imbued with the 'stiff upper-lip syndrome' of beliefs that held that:

Emotions are a sign of weakness.

Emotions are irrational and therefore not to be trusted or taken any notice of.

Emotions are childish.

Strength is about rising above my emotions.

Talking about feelings is self-centred.

As a child, Gai was frequently told to 'grow up' whenever she did something gleeful and child-like, such as laughing uproariously if someone burped loudly, or contributing to adult conversations with a piece of half-baked child perception. Any display of anger was met with comments like 'There's no need to carry on like that' or 'Watch yourself, young lady' or 'Control yourself or heaven only knows what will happen' or 'Stop over-reacting!'

Carol had heard similar injunctions. A frequent expression in her house had been 'Let's be rational about this', especially when she was upset. While Gai was encouraged to be 'a young lady', Carol was rewarded with praise and attention for her academic achievements.

While there is nothing wrong with encouraging our children to behave graciously and appropriately, or to achieve very well, if these approaches are combined with programming that gives the message 'Don't feel', as was the case with both Gai and Carol, the consequence is an ongoing experience of guilt, because we do feel all the time. With a core belief of 'Feelings are not important' both Gai and Carol had spent their lives in a state of emotional denial, Carol getting her 'goodies' of love, approval and attention through her career and Gai through being the ultimate Ms Nice Girl.

Gai's beliefs program went something like this: 'If I'm strong (interpreted as "able to rise above my emotions"), busy and capable (interpreted as "getting on with the tasks of life and not wasting my time dwelling on negative emotion") and helpful to others (interpreted as "solving their problems for them or telling them how to solve their problems"), then I am being loving and I will be loved'.

Seldom there for herself, Gai was consequently unreal and unreachable in relationships. Her task orientation meant the people in her life came second in terms of time allocated to relating. This was a direct reflection of her inner relationships, of the way she, as her now-self, ignored the voice of her child-within.

Our inner critical parent speaks the very same messages as did our external parents. In her self-talk, if Gai's emotional self — her child-within — voiced a negative emotion, such as 'I feel anxious', quick as a flash the next thought to go through her mind would be 'Pull yourself together!' or 'Just get on with it!'. This was the voice of her critical inner-parent, and was a direct echo of the former voice of her own outer parent. Similarly, if her inner-child voiced a need, such as 'I need more affection, more cuddles', back would snap her critical inner-parent, 'That's not important. There's work to do'.

Gai's attempts at helpfulness too frequently disempowered others, since she gave the message that they were not competent enough to solve their own problems, and her concept of emotional strength left her feeling empty and exhausted. Using the exercises in Part Three, she visualised herself as a child caught in the dilemma of having to deny her own feelings and needs and saw a little girl's sense of emptiness and guilt at her own feelings. At this recognition, Gai felt angry.

As the mask peeled away, the tears came with the truth — her marriage was a sham, a good front, a safety net. There was no sharing of self from either party, because she had chosen a partner who was never there and didn't know how to show his feelings either.

Denial of their emotions was the root of that 'something missing' that both Gai and Carol talked about. The need they felt to 'come alive' was actually a need to feel their emotions and to express them. Gai's anger was healthy because it provided the surge of energy required to effect change.

> **When we deny our emotions it is equivalent to lopping off our arms and legs — we are half a person, not whole.**

To start on this process of change, Carol and Gai each embarked on a retrieval mission, retrieval of the emotional self — the child-within — and reinstatement of her in her rightful place of equal importance with the rational self. Through regular self-parenting they learnt to trust their feelings and to understand that they would not be swamped by them or lose their well-developed rationality, nor would their future decisions be dominated by emotion. Rather, future decisions could be made so as to satisfy both aspects of themselves, their head and their heart, rather than head at the expense of heart which would leave them feeling half-satisfied and not knowing why.

> **We must learn to listen to our emotional self, our child-within, with unconditional acceptance.**

As they worked towards a better inner balance by doing their self-parenting with all the dedication and commitment they had formerly poured into keeping the lid on their emotions, they began to experience the sense of exhilaration and zest for life that only a free child-within can bring. They saw for themselves the beneficial effects this had on others in their lives who were now able to move closer to them. A friend of Gai's confided to her that she felt as though an invisible barrier between them had been removed. Her husband began to take a renewed interest in this fun-loving woman he found himself married to. Perhaps in time he too will regain his lost inner-child and learn to value his own needs and feelings so that their marriage might grow in depth of intimacy and sharing.

Gai's self-talk changed from critical to accepting and nurturing. For example, an 'I'm anxious' message was now met with a nurturing parent response such as 'Oh! What would you like me to do about that?'

As Carol learnt to value and trust her feelings, she was able to let her husband know how she really felt about his betrayal — angry, wounded, scared of losing him. Their former relationship was based on mutual interests, and they both needed more than that, the intimacy that comes only from the open and accepting exchange of feelings, both joys and sorrows. Hopefully he will see that his searching outside the marriage was probably motivated by the very same lack, and his own subconscious needs to come alive and feel.

It is absolutely vital to our emotional health and happiness that we accept that our feelings just *are*; that by their very nature they are often not logical and should not be expected to be; and that they often come from our past experiences, our emotional baggage.

Gina
'There is something wrong with me'

The story of Gina shows the effects of emotional denial beliefs combined with trauma in childhood. Gina's adored older sister died when Gina was four, and the message from her family came through loud and clear: 'The way to deal with this is to not dwell on it but to understand she is happy with God'. Trying to be helpful, relatives often said to her, 'Don't be sad'. Being as young as she was, she had no way of rationalising herself out of her emotions, and so she became alternately angry and depressed, creating 'fuss' and 'drama' regularly.

Her mother, desperate for relief from this constant display of emotion, often implored — her eyes raised heavenwards, her head shaking from side to side — 'Oh, Gina! Whatever is the matter with you?'

Unable to discuss her feelings, Gina was overwhelmed by her sorrow, confusion and fear of what life might deal her next. A sense of inner panic soon took hold, for she heard her mother's plea 'Oh, Gina! Whatever is the matter with you?' as 'There is something wrong with you'. She quickly became hypersensitive to real or imagined criticism, constantly alert for so much as a frown in her direction. She learnt to keep all that sense of being overwhelmed at bay in the way commonly practised by human beings — she began projecting her fears outwards and saw 'something the matter' with everyone else. As a result of this surface belief, she felt constantly angry.

Needless to say, adult life didn't work too well for Gina. Her personal relationships and her work involvements were unsatisfying to her. It was after the bitter break-up of a second marriage that Gina was driven to seek help.

She began to look inwards in personal development courses, all of which helped by allowing her space to express her rage and then her grief. But it was not until she discovered how to work with her self-talk by self-parenting that she was able to hear the deepest fear of her terrified child-within — 'There is something wrong with me' — and begin to re-educate her to truly believe, 'There is nothing the matter with me.'

Her child-within was, of course, starving for the message that 'You are absolutely fine just the way you are'. Gina's inner-child was incredulous at first, but the more Gina understood what had happened to her, the more she was able to take it on board. She was able to ask her new friends to constantly reinforce the new belief for her.

This is one of the great joys of doing one's personal growth and healing in small groups. The support for each other becomes tremendously valuable in the healing and change process.

Gina's story demonstrates very clearly the value of going with so-called negative emotions. We prefer to call them uncomfortable emotions. In other words, if we listen unconditionally to our inner-child's uncomfortable emotions, she will relax, open to us and disclose her fears and limiting beliefs.

Even uncomfortable emotions are positive because they lead us to our limiting beliefs and unmet needs.

Fear always lies under any uncomfortable emotion, and it too must be followed and not repressed. As F. D. Roosevelt knew, 'The only thing to fear is fear itself', because it keeps us trapped in its painful web, limited by the limiting beliefs which are its very source.

Lisa
'I don't matter much'

The emotion that probably has more beliefs programs associated with it than any other is anger. Some of the beliefs we can hold about anger are these:

Nice people don't show anger!

Anger is dangerous!

Anger is sinful.

I never feel anger.

Others cause my anger!

The fact is that anger itself is not dangerous / not nice / sinful, but what we might choose to do with it can be all of those things. Violence is not the result of anger, but the result of not knowing what to do with it. In how many news reports have we read or heard about the nice, quiet man who never said boo to anyone, who suddenly went on a murderous rampage? People who have 'nice, quiet' beliefs often repress their anger and the needs that this anger is alerting them to.

Many of us suppress our anger — Carol and Gai are typical examples of people who suppress anger. Then there was Lisa, who had learnt early in her life to be 'good and quiet' to please her mum. While she behaved that way, she gave some comfort to her mum and some respite from the violence and verbal abuse of her father.

As a child, Lisa experienced anger as being dangerous and destructive and obviously deeply believed that 'anger is dangerous'.

She too was an anger-suppressor. At thirty-five years of age she found herself married to an extremely difficult man, without a satisfying career of her own, and without much joy in life. She felt alternately anxious and depressed.

Lisa came to the course to help her get to the bottom of these beliefs so that she could make some changes in her life. She talked to the group about her difficult childhood and listened to their feedback:

Lisa, if I were you I'd believe that women can't expect much from life.

Lisa, if I were you I'd feel powerless.

Lisa, if I were you I'd believe life's not much fun.

Lisa, if I were you I'd believe my needs don't matter much.

As Lisa and the group assimilated this feedback, the belief lurking at the core of these branch beliefs gradually became apparent to everyone. Lisa herself finally stated it. Her face was white and her eyes were wide as she blinked several times, as though clearing away the blur of a lifetime. She took a deep breath, held it a while, sighed and whispered, 'I don't matter very much'.

A core belief that has kept energy, or emotions, frozen in the body is not going to be changed unless the body can begin to release that energy.

With such a core belief, Lisa's life was destined to be painful. What was most helpful to her at this stage was to encourage energy flow — the flow of emotions, and especially anger — in her body. She experienced a sense of enormous relief during the energy exercises when for the first time she was free to hurl anger at this whole appalling beliefs program of hers.

In the workshop, Lisa was given a phone book and asked to let it represent her limiting programming. The experience of freely hurling 'No! No! No!' at her programming and shredding the entire phone book was the start of her road to recovery. 'It gave me the chance to see it for what it was — just some insane beliefs program that had been destroying my life. I really ripped into that phone book!

Afterwards I had this sense of power and freedom I have never felt before.'

We move forward on two feet: experience and knowledge. In other words, it isn't enough to know in our heads what the problem is — to know what the beliefs program is. Personal change cannot

To be free it is necessary to express the unexpressed.

take permanent hold if we approach it solely as an intellectual exercise. To be free of our limiting beliefs and the uncomfortable emotions they cause, we must, sooner or later, permit the child-within to express everything she once was not free to express. We simply have to allow her to 'answer back' verbally, and to hurl some energy against the energy invested in her limiting beliefs. To be free of our limiting beliefs, it is necessary to assert oneself over them, energetically.

The work of reprogramming has to be undertaken with a loving attitude towards oneself, because it involves switching our inner conversations from ridicule and contempt whenever we find ourselves acting out of the old program, towards understanding and re-education instead. This happens quite easily once we have established experiential contact with our inner-child, following it with good self-parenting skills. There is no quick-fix, but neither need the change take years.

Lisa discovered, by unconditionally listening to her inner-child — her emotional self — that she was actually afraid to let go of her belief that 'I don't matter much'. In the same self-defeating way that many of us are attached to our limiting beliefs, Lisa's inner-child had reckoned very early in life that 'Dad's the one who has the power around here, and he's dangerous. Therefore power is dangerous'. And now she felt that if she gave up 'not mattering' she'd be powerful, and that was not good.

Our inner-child can feel it is unsafe to let go of a limiting belief.

So, as many of us find, Lisa had to pay special attention to re-educating her inner-child, to make it safe for her to let go of her crippling belief. You will find some background to this typical dilemma, together with exercises for dealing with it, on pages 119–122.

Lisa was well established in her healthier beliefs program within three months. As a way of beginning to learn to value her own needs and feelings, she chose to have the support of regular counselling sessions, and within twelve months she had moved out of her unworkable marriage and was studying in a field that interested her. She was also working at a part-time job which she enjoyed and which had given her the opportunity to make friends with whom she was learning to have fun.

It was then that another core belief emerged. For as Lisa began to enjoy a circle of friends, she found herself facing difficulties in these new relationships. She often felt hurt by her new friends over some interaction or other, and whenever she tried to speak with them about her feelings it seemed to her they made light of them and changed the subject to something brighter.

It all came to a head one evening when she was with one of the most valued of these friends, Laura, whom Lisa had met on the original personal change course she had taken. When Laura explained that she would not be able to keep a previous agreement with Lisa to go to a particular event together, Lisa found herself launching into a stern lecture about trust and reliability.

Fortunately, since Laura had learnt about limiting beliefs being the cause of our inappropriate behaviours and negative feelings, she managed to stay calm and simply said, 'You sound really angry with me'. Lisa was taken aback, but for the first time in her life, she owned up to the feeling of anger. Remembering what she had learnt, and encouraged by her friend, she allowed herself to go with the feeling and vocalise the thoughts that went with it. As she permitted her inner-child a free rein she heard loud and clear the belief 'Others are out to get me and always let me down'. She realised that this belief made her perceive Laura's perfectly reasonable and well-timed explanation for not being able to keep a future arrangement, as Laura letting her down and being unreliable.

Lisa knew that if she didn't change this limiting belief, she would never be able to sustain lasting relationships, so she set about employing her recently acquired knowledge and skills to effect the change. Had Lisa kept this belief she would go on being unable to see relationship situations clearly. She would never be able to distinguish between when someone was being truly unreliable or in some way attacking her, and when they were simply and appropriately communicating how things were for them in any situation.

> **Our limiting beliefs distort our perception of reality and become self-fulfilling prophecies.**

Many people who have suffered emotional or physical violence have this belief that others are out to get them and not to be trusted because sooner or later they will somehow betray them. If it is not uncovered and dealt with it can seriously undermine their progress by leading them sooner or later to distrust anyone attempting to help them.

Brian
'I have to be in control'

Brian definitely 'wore the pants' in his family. His wife and children knew that it was futile to argue with him, that he was quick to anger, and so they coped with this in their various ways. So as to avoid arguments, his wife Pamela quietly went about her own business, being careful not to involve her husband.

His relationship with his teenage children was turbulent and the more he insisted on things being done his way, the more they rebelled, until finally his sixteen-year-old daughter left school so that she could get a job and move out of home. At this, Pamela abandoned her usually compliant role and in anger and pain threatened to leave too unless Brian did something about his overbearing ways.

Brian was also 'boss' at work. Managing director of his own manufacturing business, he employed twenty-three people and ran the show as though it were an army. He paid everyone well and in return he expected loyalty and compliance. He simply could not understand his high staff turnover, which was causing serious continuity problems and threatening production levels.

Home and work seemed to him to be conspiring against him and he became angrier and more dogmatic. He was convinced that if everyone just did things his way, all would run smoothly.

It was Pamela who finally came for help, knowing that Brian would never admit to needing anything. She wanted to know what drove Brian and if there was anything she could do to make him understand that he was destroying his own world. Sadly, one cannot change another person and it is futile to try, unless that person wants help in order to change.

Pamela explained that Brian's childhood had been rough. She had stayed with him because she understood he'd had to battle his way in a largely hostile environment and had survived by sheer determination and by his own actions. Indeed, it was his apparent confidence in himself that drew her to him in the first place. Pamela saw very easily that what was driving her husband were beliefs like 'I have to be in control', and an unmet childhood need for respect.

> We all gain pay-offs from our limiting beliefs. These pay-offs must be faced and our inner-child must be convinced it is safe to let go of the beliefs.

Armed with her new insight, she decided to return home and try to reach her husband on this deeper level. Such a challenge would involve first getting Brian to see his beliefs program and the behaviour patterns it had created in him, and then he would have to be willing to work to change them. His biggest challenge, should he so decide, would be to convince his inner-child, the fighter, that it was safe to let go of his belief about having to be in control all the time. Brian may go on to alienate himself completely and find himself in a lonely, sad place — a frequent consequence of insisting on holding onto our limiting beliefs.

It is a sad fact that many of us need to hit rock-bottom before we will admit that things are not right with us and we are willing to reach out for help. This is partly because of society's pressures on us to be seen to be always coping, happy and successful. Instead we need a more realistic and humane attitude.

Everyone at some time or another goes through periods of not coping very well with the myriad of pressures from both within and without, and it is sensible and mature to reach out for appropriate support at such times. This tendency to not reach out soon enough is also a result of the fact that, until very recently, effective and appropriate professional help has simply not been as readily available as it is now.

Steven and Carmen
'If I let anyone too close they will take me over' vs 'I have to be totally one with someone else to be whole'

The threat of relationship breakdown is often a catalyst for personal change. Steven and Carmen had felt they had the world at their feet when they married six years before. They looked forward to building a happy life together.

Steven was confident, forthright, and successful in his career. A recent promotion meant that he was the youngest person to have reached that level of management in the large company for which he worked. His old school friends found it hard to conceal their envy at his meteoric rise through the ranks, but Steven laughed off the odd comment from them when they met for their regular football game on the weekend.

The shock for Steven came when Carmen announced that she was thinking of leaving him. He was becoming more and more unavailable to her, she told him, and all he cared about was his work.

'I can't understand her,' Steven protested. 'Here I am doing my hardest to build a solid financial base for us to raise a family and she turns on me. She just doesn't seem as motivated as I am, and she certainly doesn't appreciate what I'm doing.'

At the core of Steven's behaviour and approach to life lay two

> When a relationship is in difficulties there is a conflicting combination of core beliefs between the people involved.

beliefs: 'If I achieve I'll be loved and appreciated' (a legacy of a financially successful father) and 'If I let anyone too close they will take me over' (a legacy of an over-protective mother).

Carmen had an opposing program. The fifth of eight children, she jostled for the care and attention that she felt had always eluded her. Both her parents were taken up with the financial strain of so many mouths to feed, and her older siblings were too busy studying and working at part-time jobs themselves to give her any attention.

As a child, Carmen would dream of being special to someone — romantic stories appealed to her, and she imagined the joy of merging with the man of her dreams. Not only had she decided that 'I'll never be happy until I am the centre of someone else's world', but her core belief was 'I have to be totally one with someone else to be whole'.

So here were two people whose beliefs programs, seen in the harsh light of everyday life together, clashed significantly. To live together in any sort of harmony they would have had to work on those beliefs.

It often happens when relationships are in difficulty that one partner feels that it is necessary for the other person to change if the relationship is to continue. While it is ideal that both partners work on their limiting beliefs, change can often be effected by just one partner making changes. Relationships are rather like a game of tennis, where each player knows the other's game, their strengths and weaknesses, and plays to them. If one player changes the way he or she plays the game, the other player has to change in response.

If, for instance, Carmen changed her belief and became more self-reliant, she would not experience Steven as quite so unavailable to her. If Steven changed his belief about not allowing others to come too close to him, he would become more available to Carmen. Among the options open to Steven and Carmen were that they both worked on change, or just one of them did, or that they separated.

To part and to try again in a new relationship only means that each person takes those same painful and limiting beliefs into the next relationship. While they might have found new partners whose limiting beliefs would dovetail more neatly with their own, without any change in beliefs, Steven would never find intimacy and Carmen would never find herself.

Meg
'I must be cautious — life is not safe'

Meg was forty-five, had been married to Tom since she was twenty-two, and was the mother of two adult daughters. She was an introspective person. Slow to insist on her own needs being considered, she was patient, circumspect and diplomatic, qualities which served her well in her part-time job as a receptionist. But these very qualities also made her hesitant and resistant to change, so that she approached opportunities with reserve and avoided challenges whenever possible.

She was bored with her job and had been thinking for years about leaving. Her conversation was peppered with expressions like 'Better safe than sorry', 'One step at a time', and 'Fools rush in'. There was always a sense of holding back about Meg, of stifled enthusiasm and spontaneity, which we know from Gai and Carol's stories is a symptom of a stifled child-within.

Meg also suffered with back problems and low energy levels, so that she was frequently incapacitated and consequently depressed. Years of searching for a solution to her problems within both the standard and alternative medical fields had led essentially nowhere. No-one was able to find the cause of her physical distress.

Each new approach she tried, she greeted with an initial cautious hopefulness, never quite letting go of her innate scepticism. This would be followed by a period of strict adherence to the suggested regime, and some gains in either a lessening of the frequency of her back troubles or an increase in energy. For a time she would feel better, only to have the back pain return and with it lethargy and depression.

Meg greeted the suggestion that her beliefs program might be a basic contributing factor with her usual scepticism and reserve. However, being willing to 'try anything' in her search for answers, she joined a course group.

Two of her limiting beliefs were 'Nothing works for me' and 'I must always be cautious because life is not safe'. They had grown out of a childhood with too much chaos. It was obvious to everyone in her group how these two beliefs were very likely causes of her troubles. 'I must always stay safe' led to her lack of assertiveness, repression of her true needs and feelings, and her way of never committing herself totally to any enterprise in case it didn't work out. This belief was an obvious likely cause of the enormous tension in her musculature, which she had been holding taut since childhood in order to restrain her feelings and keep her fears of life at bay. 'Nothing works for me' meant nothing was going to fix her problems ... especially not herself! Meg was caught in a catch-22 situation.

> **Our limiting beliefs can cause physical problems.**

Meg set to work to change other beliefs first — the belief that 'I'm not very important' was the first one she worked on. The last we heard of Meg, her self-assurance had improved and she was being more assertive with her family. She had finally taken a risk and left her job. She found another which was more stimulating and challenging for her. We trust that as she fully integrates her new belief that 'I matter' she will continue to seize opportunities more fully, and to welcome challenges instead of hiding from them because of her fearful beliefs.

Meg could now step even more fully into her own power by changing the belief that 'Nothing works for me' to one that might allow the next medical approach she tries to work for her. Or perhaps as she replaces the beliefs that cause her to hold her musculature in a permanent state of tension, her back problems will disappear, though she would do well with the help of a form of therapy such as massage or yoga to facilitate the release of such long-held physical tension.

Kerry
'If I fit in with others, they should be there for me'

An easy, happy childhood is no sure guarantee of a smooth and satisfying adulthood. Kerry's story is a good illustration of this fact.

Kerry was an attractive woman with three children. She worked as a secretary and there was no shortage of work for her. However, what bothered her was the series of unsuccessful relationships she'd had, including a divorce.

Her childhood had been a particularly happy one, and she had loved her parents dearly, having found it quite easy as a child to adapt to their easy-going attitude. She had learnt the rule of fitting in with others and the rewards of that — her parents adored her, often telling their friends how 'blessed' they had been with this perfect child.

But as an adult, Kerry was having trouble understanding why others did not respond as her parents had, and she found that instead men responded to her extreme adaptability with betrayal or anger. The problem for Kerry was that she had become a chameleon, always accommodating others but losing herself in the process. Her relationships were not built on two people each seeing who the other truly was and deciding if their attitudes, interests, philosophy of life, or even their needs, coincided so as to make a meaningful relationship possible.

Rather, her relationships were built on two people being attracted to each other and one of them immediately moving to adapt to the other's way of being and expecting to be eternally loved for doing so. Kerry had learnt as a child that 'If I fit in with others, they should be there for me'.

But in denying her true self so much she inevitably felt resentful, especially when her partner was not as compliant as she was. Kerry

> Change depends on our willingness to take on the responsibility for our own life's outcomes.

would feign interest in TV programs that she did not really enjoy, and attend sporting events which bored her stiff. She held the dual beliefs that resentors hold: 'Nice people don't show anger' and 'Others should … (be there for me)'. Inherent in Kerry's core belief and in the resentment she felt was the attitude that others were responsible for her happiness. It takes courage to change such a life pattern.

As is true of all beliefs, Kerry's beliefs clouded her ability to actually see clearly. She was not looking to see who the men she met really were, because she believed that they were / would be / should be there for her as long as she acted in a certain way. The initial decision to enter into a relationship was taken on a superficial reading of the person and as each one in turn did not 'measure up', she could easily discard him, saying: 'He was totally self-centred. He didn't care at all for me'.

> Under limiting beliefs lie unmet needs.

What was Kerry really needing? What were the needs that were going unmet, causing her so much unhappiness and disillusionment? Kerry had the basic human needs for love, recognition and companionship, but like all limiting beliefs, hers were making it extremely difficult for her to meet those needs.

When we carry beliefs such as Kerry's, we are deeply attached to the idea that 'others' or 'life' is responsible for our misery and, paradoxically, we derive satisfaction from the feeling of resentment we carry around with us. It shields us from having to assume full responsibility for our lives, although we may have convinced ourselves that we are responsible. After all, as Kerry saw it, she was always the one making all the effort, the one left with responsibility for her children.

In a sense, those beliefs are right — others and life often did visit unmanageable things upon us when we were little, or we did form beliefs like Kerry's that are childish and prevent us from growing up. But we are no longer children, and to hold onto this resentment keeps us from growing up. Perhaps when we make a habit of blaming others we see the only alternative as being to blame ourselves.

The answer lies in stepping out of the blame framework altogether and seeing our beliefs for what they are — beliefs rather than reality. From there we can assume our own power to change them. It is then that we find ourselves in the marvellous position of being able to see clearly and able to create our outcomes in life the way we truly want them. This does not mean that an individual must be a self-sufficient island. Rather, a person's needs include the need for intimacy and relationship.

I alone am responsible for meeting my unmet needs.

If Kerry faced her resentment and her blame of others, and the limiting belief which is creating both whilst leaving her miserable and disillusioned, she could change the limiting belief 'Others should be there for me if I fit in with them' to 'I act only in ways that are true to myself and I am responsible for my choice of an appropriate life partner'. The blame would then stop and she would assume her full personal power to create her own outcomes in life — there would no longer be any cause for the resentment.

Personal power is my ability to act appropriately to get my needs met.

When we step outside of the blame framework and into the responsibility arena we immediately perceive that wherever we place responsibility, there also we place our power. So, in stepping into self-responsibility, we step away from a sense of powerlessness. Operating at this level of responsibility and power in turn creates value for others in our relationships.

Whenever I act appropriately to meet my own needs I create value for others in the process.

Taking appropriate action means acting or communicating without trespassing on anyone else's rights to respect and fulfilment. For instance,

Kerry would create enormous value for the men in her life by not entering into inappropriate relationships in the first place — something you may recall Cathy, the architect in Part One, came to realise.

Barbara
'Life wasn't meant to be a bed of roses'

Barbara was a woman in her mid-forties who had been feeling depressed for some time. The reason, she said, was that she worked in an air-conditioned, fluorescent-lit, old stone building, and by the end of each workday she felt low no matter how much she had managed to achieve that day.

'It's like a dungeon in there,' Barbara said. 'It's dark and dingy — sometimes I feel like running out screaming. I love fresh air, and what I love most is working on bush regeneration or in my garden. But working where I do is just deadly for me.'

Taking responsibility for the unmet needs that lie beneath our uncomfortable emotions means hearing such messages from ourselves and doing something about them. Put in self-parenting terms, it means that we listen to our child-within and then take responsibility for doing something out there in the world to fix things.

Of course, this is where limiting beliefs might get in our way. 'I'm powerless' or 'My needs don't matter' or 'Life wasn't meant to be a bed of roses' would have stopped Barbara from taking any such remedial action.

By listening to her inner-child, and with acceptance of the need for and commitment to change, she can decide to do something to change her situation. The actual workplace changes she might have made could range through a host of options from changing careers to brightening up her office herself or enlisting her employer's cooperation.

One thing is certain: if Barbara's beliefs had caused her to think 'I shouldn't complain, at least I've got a job. There's nothing I can do about it — the windows are tiny and that's that!' then she would have stayed depressed, and as a consequence her family would have suffered, her work would have continued to suffer, and the negativity would have spread wherever she went.

In other words, unless she took responsibility for changing something so she met her own needs and thus felt better, she was not creating value for anyone else either. In Barbara's own words, 'As far as I was concerned, there was no option but to change. I did feel the burden of having to provide for the family, but I knew that was no excuse to continue in a situation that was causing me so much unhappiness and frustration. Nobody at home was happy with my being the way I was, and I was totally miserable. I was bringing home the bacon all right, but it was tainted bacon.

'What I did was apply for several other positions and I was offered one that offered as much pay but not the same intellectual stimulation as the one I already had. All these doubts started whirring away in my head: Stay with what you know / Why do you want change at this time of your life? / Stop complaining and get on with it … that sort of thing.

'The big advantages of the new position were that I would be working in a light, airy building and there were opportunities for advancement eventually. I did some thorough listening to myself before I decided to take the new job and apply myself to gaining rapid promotion.'

Gordon
'Others come first'

Children who are too soon placed in a position of responsibility inevitably learn to minimalise the importance of their own needs and feelings. Gordon was one such person. At thirty-six he felt trapped in his job as a human resources manager with a large firm; he confided, 'My wife is complaining that I've become dull and boring. She thinks I don't love her any more because I'm just not interested in doing all the things we usually do together. I've tried to explain that I do love her, but I've just run out of go. Life seems flat and I can't work up any enthusiasm for much at all. There must be something wrong with me because I've got a good family life and a good job and enough money, but I'm not sparking'.

His father had left the family when Gordon was seven, and stepping into the role of 'little man of the house', Gordon quickly took on the belief that 'I have to be good and strong and protect others — others come first'. However, as he was only seven years old, the burden of this decision was enormous. As often happens in such circumstances, Gordon struggled to put his own needs and feelings second, believing this to be the correct and necessary thing to do, only to be constantly troubled by needs and feelings that would not go away. The child Gordon then struggled to make sense of this inner conflict, finally doing so by deciding he was not a truly good person because he could not do what he believed he must — conquer his own needs and feelings. The consequence of this belief that 'I am not truly a good person' was the core emotion of guilt.

As Gordon went through life, he felt guilty whenever he did something for himself; guilty whenever he needed support, encouragement, consideration or an expression of appreciation or affection; guilty on those odd occasions when he expressed his own preferences. He felt good about himself only when he was giving these things to others and he had made a career out of doing just this in the human resources field. In fact he spent so much of his working time in the role of company counsellor that there was little time left to tackle the broader management issues that were his responsibility.

While doing his beliefs-clarification work Gordon allowed his inner-child, his emotional/historical self, to speak more and more openly about his feelings and needs back then when he was a child struggling to take on so much responsibility. He built a clear understanding of this child-within who, he discovered, was still very much alive inside himself; he came to fully accept and appreciate the dilemma this child had faced; he developed an emotional bond with this inner-child; and as he did these things, the guilt ebbed away and in its place grew a determination to respect his own natural needs and feelings.

In order to change, you must pay attention to the origins of your limiting beliefs.

Once he understood that it was vital to pay the same wonderful attention to himself as he so well knew how to give to others, he took to the task of changing his beliefs with business-like precision. On his desk he put a picture of himself as a child, a constant reminder of his first responsibility. He wrote himself an affirmation that read, 'I am a good person and my needs and feelings are natural and important'. He asked his wife to ask him every day before they left for work what he most wanted to do for himself today and to ask him every evening at dinner time whether he had done it.

Gordon was able to effect a profound change in his life in a short space of time. Like Gai and Carol, Gordon discovered his energy and zest for living returning rapidly once he began to give his own needs and feelings their rightful place in his life. His wife was delighted.

Within weeks he felt quite differently about his job and his emphasis within it shifted gears. He began to combine an assertiveness that had only occasionally surfaced before, with his excellent listening skills and his great ability to empathise with others. His colleagues were stunned, then relieved, when he decided on a point of view and communicated it plainly, confident that his views should be included in their search for solutions and clear policy directions. Previously they had known he would always bend to accommodate them and privately they voiced their frustration with what they perceived as his lack of management skills. Within two months his managing director was congratulating him on some bold new initiatives he had introduced, argued for and shepherded through management meetings.

In ignoring his own needs and feelings Gordon had been ignoring his first responsibility — himself — and his inner-child had responded finally by withholding energy, joy and enthusiasm.

The more carefully we attend to our own needs and feelings, the more loving and productive we become. This inner focus leads not to selfishness and navel-gazing, but to more energy, and a greater ability to contribute to the lives of others in positive ways. We simply cannot go on giving when our own cup is running dry.

Finally, there are some important points to be made about guilt. The guilt Gordon had felt was destructive guilt — guilt irrationally taken on as part of one's emotional baggage. This kind of guilt usually begins to subside when we allow ourselves to perceive clearly our innocent inner-child's original predicament.

There is, however, constructive guilt — the guilt that tells us we have transgressed our own moral code and consequently instructs us to change our behaviour. It is important to distinguish between the two types, especially if guilt is your frequent companion.

Dan
'No problems!'

The emphasis in Dan's family was summed up in the attitude 'We don't have any of *that* (conflict) around here'. The levels of denial were quite high, given that his dad was an alcoholic, a situation which his mother habitually explained away with comments such as 'Dad's in one of his funny states tonight'.

Dad's 'funny state' meant he had drunk excessively on the way home from work and could hardly keep awake at the dinner table. He was never violent and always remained agreeable.

Dan learnt to be similarly unrealistic about both his own problems and his own feelings, avoiding negative feelings by escaping into his head and becoming rational, focussed and cool.

Now in his late thirties, Dan was shocked that his life, which he had always described as 'charmed', had fallen apart. His wife had left him and taken the children. He had no understanding of why this might have happened since, he said, 'There had never been any problems at all'. His belief was that 'There can be no problems in my life' and it had seen him through to thirty-eight years of age.

This would seem to be a great belief and the pay-offs for holding onto it are obvious. But it simply doesn't work because problems and difficulties are an integral part of life. They give us the opportunity to learn and grow if we can only uncover the best way to approach them.

The opposite view to Dan's would be that 'Life is one huge unsolvable problem' — a basic belief of the classic Victim who finds it difficult to see a way out of any difficulty. What we need is a perception of problems that is balanced and healthy and works for us.

A belief that 'There is no such thing as a problem without a gift for me in its hand' is one that makes life a lot easier, provided we know how to find the gift in each problem we face.

Needless to say, a belief in 'No problems here' involves extraordinary levels of emotional denial, and Dan's bind was a difficult one, because it would have involved admitting first to problems and then to the feelings of desperation he had carried since childhood. This was too difficult for Dan, who insisted that it was his wife who had the problems and that she should seek help.

For someone like Dan who was such an exclusively rational person, time with a bodywork therapist would be invaluable in helping him release the blocked energy in his body. When we are very disconnected from our emotions, the feelings are blocked in our bodies, as we discussed in Part One.

Until someone like Dan can become aware of these feelings, he can't be fully aware of the pain his beliefs are causing him. He will continue to live in a state of emotional denial, never understanding why others move away from him or why he finds it difficult to form genuine, loving relationships.

The importance of being aware of needs and feelings is particularly evident in the area of conflict resolution. It would seem obvious that most of us would like to resolve conflict successfully in order to live more peaceful and harmonious lives. However, many people have great difficulty in learning the communication skills necessary and in accepting that conflict can be resolved to the benefit of all.

The attitudes and skills required for resolving conflict can often be assimilated only after core beliefs are changed.

What stand in the way are beliefs programs. Someone like Gordon, who retained his core belief that he was not important, found taking on assertiveness skills all but impossible. Allan, with his perfectionist beliefs, could not accept the idea that mistakes could be regarded as learning opportunities, an attitude basic to good conflict resolution.

One of the greatest hurdles to healthy conflict resolution within families is the 'Don't rock the boat' attitude, the 'Anything for a peaceful life' approach, which leads to problems being swept under the carpet and the careful avoidance of conversations that involve the airing of differences. The only permissible conversations are generally those of the information-swapping type, with any attempt to move into deeper reflective or analytical levels abruptly terminated.

Anyone who won't play by the rules becomes the family scapegoat, the one who 'obviously' rocks the boat and so 'causes all the problems'. Instead of effort going into conflict resolution, it goes into developing more subtle evasion tactics and covert agreements about what's 'wrong' with the scapegoat. The family will often tend to move away from such a person, leaving them marginalised or totally ostracised.

Sally, Denise and Simon
'There's nothing I can do'

Quite different from Dan are those people who are not only in touch with their feelings, but swamped by them. They tend to hold beliefs like:

Life is unfair!

No matter what I do, I never get what I need or want.

Others always let me down.

There is never enough for me.

Life just happens to me.

What happens to me is beyond my control.

It doesn't take enormous insight to see that such 'Victim beliefs' can form during a particularly difficult childhood — usually during a childhood involving trauma and/or chaos.

Sally experienced a nagging sense of apathy as a result of such a beliefs program which she formed during a childhood where she was often left to amuse herself without an adequately stimulating environment. 'Life is boring and there is nothing I can do to change it' is what Sally believed.

An ingrained sense of powerlessness underlies all such Victim beliefs and frequently results in depression as it had for Denise, whose mother had been seriously ill for much of her early childhood.

Denise's life had been one of unstable relationships. Because she had difficulty trusting anyone to nurture and support her consistently, she would become clinging and dependent as soon as a relationship began. Inevitably, the new man in her life would back off very quickly.

She had lived with a man whom she regarded as 'a rock', only to discover that rocks are hard and cold and unaccommodating. When this relationship became violent she limped away, broken and suicidal.

Denise was fortunate enough to find a good therapist and so began the long-term recovery and healing process she needed. Her first glimpse of a way out of her prison of pain and victimisation began when she saw her beliefs clearly.

'I had felt so powerless all my life,' she said later, 'and when I realised that it was only my beliefs that had kept me there, I felt strong and hopeful for the future. Growing up with your mother so terribly ill as I had, you learn to creep around the house, not bothering anyone, wishing you could make her better but knowing you are unable to. The whole house revolved around Mum and her state of health. It was as if no-one else existed there.

'With help I found that I had this core belief that life is beyond my control. I have worked on that for some time, parenting myself and learning to give myself the attention I craved and, in short, to take control of my life myself. I've found out that I have to love and nurture myself before I can expect others to do so. I was hoping one day someone would come along and make me feel good about myself. I know that that someone has to be me, so now, instead of getting lost in sad, powerless feelings, I listen to the child within me, reassuring her and actually taking action. I have never felt so powerful.'

Simon had a similar belief to Denise's — that he didn't matter much — but his history had been vastly different. Simon held such beliefs because his father left the family abruptly when Simon was five years old. He was only too aware of his feelings of anxiety. While his mother had been a stable and consistent parent to him, his father had always resisted attempts to involve him in the fathering role.

Positive thinking does not deal with the root cause of our struggles.

At twenty-four, Simon was insecure about his own abilities and found it almost impossible to assert himself effectively. He had tried positive thinking for years, telling himself he was confident, assertive, capable; but each time he failed to live up to his positive messages. This approach served only to plunge him deeper into his prevailing sense of powerlessness and to reinforce his core limiting beliefs.

'It's because I never had a role model to show me how,' he explained. 'If Dad had done what he should have done I would feel more confident about myself the way other men my age do. It's a bit late to start learning all that now.'

While Simon continued to blame his father for bad parenting he was giving into Victim beliefs — that we can't change ourselves or our circumstances because of other people. While he held his father responsible for his current unhappiness he was giving his own power away to his father and was left feeling more powerless than ever.

Although as a child Simon had hoped to engage his father and to be loved and appreciated by him, he was doing himself a disservice now as an adult to hold onto those hopes. In clarifying his beliefs —

one of which was 'I will only feel all right when Dad notices me and cares for me' — he realised that he was only hurting himself by continuing to expect parenting from a father who had consistently refused to provide it over the years.

> As with all Victim beliefs, the pay-off is that responsibility is placed elsewhere.

In deciding to take full responsibility for his own parenting, Simon solemnly promised his own inner-child to 'be there' for him as his father had not been.

This meant valuing his feelings, protecting himself by being more aware of the type of people with whom he formed friendships, and doing whatever was necessary to secure the guidance he craved. This might have involved reading helpful books, talking with friends' parents, taking an assertiveness training course and asking assertive friends to point out when he was not standing up for himself.

Simon knew that his goal was to learn to provide his own guidance from within by valuing his inner-child — his emotions — and by building up practical knowledge and parental skills.

> It is never too late to have the parents you needed — if you learn to be a good parent to yourself.

We cannot hold onto resentments and be powerful as adults. As children we may have been victims, but as adults we need not be. The difference lies in our choice of beliefs and in our willingness to learn to parent ourselves differently and more effectively.

Conclusion

Most of our parents, however inadequate they may have been, did the best that they could given their own belief systems and the damage they themselves sustained in their early lives. A great sense of freedom comes when we are able to take the final step away from blame and its attendant resentment by forgiving our parents — within ourselves — and for our own sake, not theirs. Whether or not we ever tell them our story of damage and forgiveness does not matter. The work of freedom takes place within ourselves.

As the case studies show, beliefs come in all shapes and sizes. Whatever our own particular beliefs program might be, it is certain that parts of it are limiting us and causing us to struggle unnecessarily.

In Part Three of this book we offer you the opportunity to clarify your beliefs and to work at uncovering your core limiting beliefs — the beliefs that underpin all your programming and are responsible for your struggle and pain.

Having clarified your beliefs, you can take them into Part Four to change them into beliefs that will make life much more satisfying and happy for you.

PART THREE

Clarifying Your Limiting Beliefs

Introduction

E very living being has a drive to grow, to go beyond what is. You have opened this book because of that drive. On the other hand, we are all strongly attached to remaining just as we are, in the interests of maintaining our concepts about who we are and of staying safely with what we already know about ourselves. You will most likely be aware of these conflicting pulls within you. Jung called them 'the pull back into the comfort of the womb' and 'the natural thrust into life'.

If you are reading this, you are probably contemplating undertaking the exercises that follow. You are in the grip of 'the natural thrust into life'. You are contemplating undertaking a personal change program so that you may live your life more abundantly, more joyfully, more fulfillingly. Well, congratulations! Too many of us go through life never arriving at this point, never realising that our ship is not going where we want it to until we jump aboard, hoist the sails, and start steering. But you are saying that you are actually going to get moving and do something about it. Your personal growth program has already begun!

The program

Clarifying one's limiting beliefs must be done in a way that allows us to link them to the emotions we felt when we first assimilated them. It is no use clarifying one's beliefs program as a purely intellectual exercise. Otherwise we are merely engaging in positive thinking, which we know from Part One does not usually last. To be effective and lasting, personal change *must* occur in our heads and our hearts together.

In the field of personal change, we must move forward on two feet — intellect *and* experience, head *and* heart, reason *and* emotions.

If you are like some of the people in our case studies (such as Dan) and have long ago heavily dissociated yourself from your emotions, you will need to do the self-parenting exercises centred on the child-within for longer than other people may need to. You will be able to tell if this is the case, because these exercises will seem wooden to you — that is, you will not experience a sense of 'genuine' connection with your inner-child when you do either them (Sessions 4, 5, 6) or the Guided Visualisation (Session 7).

Keeping a journal

You will find it helpful if you keep a journal in which to do the exercises. This could be a ruled pad or special notebook, of a minimum size of A4. In this book you can do all the written parts of the exercises as well as keep any notes you might want to make about your progress, or the thoughts, feelings or insights that occur to you along the way. In short, your journal is a special place where you keep everything to do with your beliefs work. This becomes a record of your progress that you can use to keep track of yourself, to look back and recall insights that were important to you at the time, to have an overview of how you proceeded through the exercises and what had particular relevance for you.

A partner to share with

Some of the exercises can be done with a partner, if the idea appeals to you. This would need to be someone you feel you can be completely open with and whom you can completely trust to respect your confidentiality. This is very much optional, as all the exercises can be done by yourself.

If you do decide to ask someone to be your sharing partner, you will want them on hand for Session 1 and it is absolutely essential that they read and understand the following brief.

Brief for partners

Your role is to simply listen when the person doing the exercises asks you to. Your job is to be a sounding board only, so that the person speaking can hear what they are saying. You will be most helpful if you restrict yourself to asking questions that help that person deepen and clarify their understanding of whatever they are talking about. You will be positively *un*helpful if you give any advice whatsoever, or make any judgements, or offer solutions, or state your own opinions or perceptions at all. The golden rule for taking this role, indeed for any true listening, is to avoid the word 'I' — unless it is to ask questions like 'I have the feeling that you're not sure about that?' or 'I'm wondering exactly what you are saying?' or 'I suspect there's more to that?' Such questions keep the focus on the person talking.

Timing

Unless otherwise stated, you will get the most from each exercise if the length of time suggested for any particular exercise is adhered to.

The nature of this program

What you get out of doing this program is directly proportional to what you put into it — that is the nature of all personal change work. We know from our own personal experience and from the experience of many people who have undertaken this program in the groups we run, that it has the potential to enable you to change your experience of life in whatever way you want. But without your energetic and committed input, it will remain just a good idea in a book.

Self-parenting
Essential background

At this point you might like to re-read pages 7–11 in Part One.

You are going to spend time for some of these sessions talking to yourself. Don't worry — it's really the sanest people who consciously talk to themselves! The rest of us just rabbit on in our own heads, giving ourselves headaches and driving ourselves loopy with the inner conflict and turmoil. The truth is we carry on conversations in our heads all the time, and learning to tune in to the nature of these conversations, to tune in to your own radio station as it were, and take control of them, is one of the most productive things you could ever learn to do.

You may find yourself being quite critical and demanding or negating and neglectful of your child-within at first. Then this is the way you talk to yourself all day, every day. Would you talk to anyone else like this so constantly? More especially, would you talk to a child, any child, like this, day in, day out? It is time to stop talking to yourself in any way other than in a loving, caring, understanding, accepting way. Or perhaps you will discover that your inner-child is running your life and needs more guidance from you.

No matter what it is you want to change within yourself, it is always the way you are parenting yourself that has to change.

You will almost certainly not make this change all at once. It will be gradual, but once you are aware of how you abuse yourself within your own mind, in your self-talk, you will certainly want to stop. We recall the look on many people's faces as it dawned on them what they had been doing to themselves all their lives. We especially recall Susan, shaking her head in stunned disbelief at the level of her abusive self-talk, murmuring wide-eyed, 'This has got to stop'. Then, with determination, 'This is *going* to stop!' For how can we possibly ever be at peace with ourselves, when we constantly abuse or ignore ourselves? If you become as determined as Susan, you will stop very quickly.

Self-parenting is not a process to be entered into lightly. It is vital that once you begin self-parenting you continue, because if you commence paying attention to and having conversations with your child-within and then ignore her, your child-within will feel even more abandoned and distrustful of you than before. This will make it more difficult to proceed in the future and your child-within can really hold you to ransom by withdrawing energy, motivation and enthusiasm from things you presently enjoy, if you are not aware of what you have done. If you do begin and then forget about it for a few days, apologise to your child-within and explain what has happened before re-starting further conversations.

If you begin these exercises and, even after following our suggestions, you find the conversations simply do not flow for you (as a small percentage of people do find), then consider this. Have you been soldiering on through life feeling mostly pain or numbness? Is it possible your child-within is so damaged she cannot trust even you enough to commence a dialogue?

If so, recognise that damaged children need professional care and find yourself a good therapist; see our guidelines on pages 11, 132 and 140. Or you could buy a book of self-parenting exercises which are specifically graded to gently coax your child-within into communicating with you; see our book references at the back of this book. But have your support network firmly in place, even if this means a therapist.

Alternatively, if you begin the self-parenting conversations and uncover an incredibly angry child inside yourself, see our suggestions for managing this anger on pages 137 and 138. If following these suggestions does not reduce your rage to manageable proportions, then it is important that you consult a therapist who can help you work through your anger to a calmer place inside yourself.

Setting up your sessions

For these sessions, specifically Sessions 4, 5, 6 and 10, you will need two chairs set up facing each other, one for you (or your now-self), and one for your child-within. We do recommend that you place a photograph of yourself as a child on one of the chairs: this is an excellent aid. Some really uninhibited people even use a cuddly toy placed on the child-within's chair. If you like the idea, try it.

Next you will find it helpful if you have a tape recorder to record your conversations. This is so you can play them back to yourself in order to hear just how you talk to yourself. It is the how that is important and there are questions at the end of some sessions to help you with this understanding. If you do not have this equipment and if it is impossible for you to borrow it, you can proceed without it.

If you find it is almost impossible to talk with your child-within fairly freely in a way that flows along even if haltingly at first, you may like to use your journal to write down whatever your child-within has to say. This means that whenever you move to the child-within's chair, you pick up the journal and start writing. Some people find doing this writing a help and some find it a hindrance. If you find it just won't work without writing, then write. Whatever works for you is the way. If you try writing and still find it impossibly difficult to get these conversations flowing, a very powerful technique is to write your child-within's part of the conversation with your non-dominant hand. That is, if you are right-handed, write with your left hand and vice versa.

Use each of the self-parenting questions as a launching pad into a conversation, back and forth between you and your child-within, until that part of your conversation comes to a natural resting place. Then move on to the next question. The questions are being asked by your now-self to your child-within. It should take you at least fifteen minutes to work through these questions.

Be sure to move back and forth between the two chairs, according to who is speaking at any given time. It is important to keep moving between the chairs. The movement keeps you focussed on the process and less likely to wander off into a reverie. It also helps make the distinction between the two aspects of yourself clearer and makes it easier to tune in to the nature of your inner relationship, which is the all-important focus. If at any stage you are not sure which part of you is speaking, don't let that stop you, just keep the conversation going until you move on to the next question from your now-self.

The conversations you are about to have, like all your internal conversations, are between you and your feelings. So when you ask a question like 'How are you doing right now, child-within?' you are checking out how things are with yourself emotionally.

Your child-within might respond with something like 'I'm OK.' To which you might respond with: 'Anything else? Will you tell me some more about feeling OK?' To which your emotional self, or child-within, might respond: 'Well, I think it's odd that you're actually asking, but I'm feeling fine. Enthusiastic about all this. A bit worried about where it's leading. But I like new things, so it's fine by me. And I enjoyed the dinner we just had by the way. I like lamb'. And so on, until you think you've 'done' that line of approach and you move on to the next question.

Session 1
Your goal
Background

It is essential that you be absolutely clear about what it is you want from this program — if you don't know, you are not going to get it. What exactly is it you want more of in your life? Remember, you cannot change another person, you can only change yourself; so be sure to frame your goal in terms of yourself. For instance, if you want a partner or a better relationship with your partner, you will be looking to change the limiting beliefs *you* hold that are stopping you from having this in your life. Remember Steven and Carmen, Kerry, and Dan in Part Two.

Aim

The purpose of this process is to state your goal in one clear sentence.

Instructions

For this session you will need your journal, a pen, an alarm or timer, and your partner (optional). You will also need colour pencils, a computer or whatever else you would like to use to make a special goal statement page for the front of your journal. Set an alarm or timer and give yourself precisely ten minutes to explore your goals, then two to five minutes to write your goal. Take as long as you like to make your special page.

Process

With your partner, or aloud to yourself, talk about 'What I want to achieve for myself from this program'. Then take two to five minutes to write your goal in one sentence. Your goal sentence should begin, 'I want to change the limiting beliefs I hold that prevent me from ...' It can be a complex sentence, but do make it only one sentence.

Now take some time to make a special page for the front of your journal, on which your goal is written in some special way — computer graphics, calligraphy, decoration with artwork or stick-ons — whatever makes it special for you. Give your goal the attention it deserves. It is a major statement. At the very least, write it in big letters on the first page of your journal.

Session 2
Learning to listen for beliefs
Background

Often we form a picture of other people simply because of the things they say. In the comments they make, in the asides and offhand remarks, a lot is revealed about who they are. We are not always aware of the process of forming a picture of others; perhaps we have a sense of it but don't quite know its origins.

If we are in the habit of understanding or summing up other people but not so good at doing it about ourselves, it's time to start practising. If we are serious about pinpointing our beliefs it is important that we learn to listen carefully to ourselves — not in a totally self-absorbed way, but in a perceptive and insightful way. Just as we pick up clues from other people, we can do the same for ourselves, noticing the little comments we make, and our responses in various circumstances.

The value in doing this is that we begin to hear exactly what program is running us. For example, hearing lots of 'musts' and 'shoulds' peppering our conversation and our thinking gives us a clue as to what our core beliefs might be. If I often hear myself saying things like 'Well, what's the point anyway?', I could possibly have a belief that 'I am powerless to change things' or 'I am ineffective'. Listening carefully to our self-talk can be very clarifying.

Aim

The purpose of this exercise is for you to practise thinking about and listening for likely beliefs.

Instructions

Here is a list of some common expressions that give away something of the beliefs program of the individuals saying them. In the adjacent column, write whatever you think the belief could be behind each statement. There is no 'correct' answer.

For the purposes of this exercise, assume that these are expressions these people use habitually. For example, if I often say 'Oh! I don't know', it's likely that I have a limiting belief about my own capabilities, a belief such as 'I'm not very clever' or 'I can't cope' or even 'Life is too confusing'. However, if I say 'Oh! I don't know' once in a blue moon, it's probably a simple statement of fact.

Process

Habitual sayings	Likely beliefs
Oh, God! I'm hopeless.	
Get it right for heaven's sake!	
Yes, but …	
What's it to you?	
Back off!	
Oh, no! Not again!	
I can't stand this.	
There's no need to cry about it.	
What you should do is …	
If you'd just … then I could …	
Well, that's just the way I am.	
What do *you* think?	
As long as you're happy …	
Near enough is not good enough!	
They always do this to me.	
Where are people when you need them?	
I shouldn't feel this way.	
Stop worrying.	
I don't need anyone.	

You can expand the list of habitual sayings yourself by beginning to listen carefully to the sorts of comments that others (and you yourself) make regularly. It takes a little practice to develop the skill of really hearing those give-away comments and linking them to a limiting belief. Start listening now as you go about your usual routine, while continuing to make your way through the following sessions.

Session 3
Getting to know your child-within
Background

While we may have long since passed from childhood to adulthood, we still hold within us the child we were — our child-within — who first formed the beliefs that cause us still to struggle with certain aspects of life. We may carry on through life unaware of this child and we may even deny that child's very existence, but our child-within is there, waiting to be acknowledged and heard.

As we said in Part One, our inner-child is also the part of us that feels, that cries, that hurts, that wants to be cared for and nurtured and protected. It is easy to understand this part of ourselves if we turn our eyes and hearts to any outer-child. The needs of our inner-child are the same as the needs of any outer-child. The fact that we have grown past childhood is no reason for us to ignore these needs or to suppose that we have left behind the child in us forever. In fact, it is because we think we have left the child behind that life can become so difficult. Some of us feel initially embarrassed at the very idea of part of us still being child-like, but this is the very part of us that holds the key to our future fulfilment and happiness. Our embarrassment is actually the result of some very limiting beliefs we have programmed into ourselves about who we have to be as adults.

We are now going to look at ways to welcome this child back into your life. For it is your inner-child who holds your limiting beliefs, the beliefs that you took on as a small child and carried into adulthood, even though they are no longer appropriate. And your inner-child clings to those beliefs because they were once so essential to her wellbeing. But we, as adults, can now distinguish which beliefs we no longer want to keep and persuade our inner-child that it is safe and beneficial to let go of any particular belief.

So here we are today, our now-self, comprising our totality as an adult, including this inner-child aspect. The now-self has a number of roles, including that of inner-parent. We now, as adults, have full responsibility for looking after the child in us; that is, for looking after our own feelings and needs. Most of us fail to do this, and yet this is precisely what we must do, and do consciously, if we are to feel content and fulfilled.

Many of us disregard the importance of our feelings and we have seen this to be the problem in many of our case studies. Others of us are simply 'lost' in our feelings, with no idea of what to do with them or we allow our feelings to control us. In all cases, we are not looking after our inner-child. Indeed, we are doing the opposite — ignoring or failing to support her.

We admonish ourselves, our child-selves, with 'shoulds' and 'oughts' and 'musts': we judge ourselves harshly. We put ourselves down, we fail to listen to ourselves, we make incredible demands upon ourselves, we criticise ourselves, we lose ourselves — all within the confines of our own minds. To change means to change this. To change means to change our relationship to ourselves.

To lead happy and fulfilling lives it is essential that we relate to our inner-child in a loving and caring way — a way that is based upon total acceptance of our inner-child. Only then can we clarify our limiting beliefs and reassure our inner-child about letting go of them. Only then do they fall away and we very quickly begin to wonder that we ever held them at all. Only then can we move into true power over our own lives — the power to create them as loving, satisfying and creative.

Aim

The purpose of the following exercise is to put you in touch with your inner-child so that the process of clarifying your limiting beliefs can begin.

Instructions

Set aside an hour or so to talk with your Listening Partner about your childhood or set aside an evening, or a minimum of two hours, and write the story of your childhood.

Whichever way you choose, you can use the following questions as prompts if you get stuck. But the idea is to just cast your mind back and talk or write about whatever pops into it — you may not need to refer to these prompts at all.

Process

Where did you live? When? With whom? Did you have any pets?

Where did you go to school? Who were your friends? Where did you play? What did you play?

Did you go on holidays? Where? With whom? What else about your holidays can you recall?

Talk about the times you enjoyed as a child.

Talk about the times that were difficult for you as a child.

Talk about any particularly vivid memories.

Session 4
Defining the nature of the relationship between you and your child-within
Background

Re-read the sections at the beginning of Part Three headed 'Essential background' on page 80, and 'Setting up your sessions' on page 81.

Aim

Your main aim for this session is to become aware of the nature of the way you talk to yourself within your own mind, day by day, minute by minute, relentlessly, unendingly.

Instructions

The conversation part of this process should take at least fifteen minutes. The replay of your tape and answering the questions that follow should take another twenty minutes. Switch on your tape recorder and sit in one of the two chairs which will be your now-self's chair.

Process

Your now-self begins:

Tell me, child-within, how are you doing right now?

What kind of day did you have today, child-within?

Do you think it's strange to be having this conversation with me?

If we could be anywhere we wanted right now, where would you choose to be?

What is one of your most favourite things to do and when did you last do it?

Will you tell me your feelings about the reasons we've decided to do this program — about the things in our life that are not the way we'd really want them to be? I'd really like to hear openly and honestly from you about all this.

Do you want to change anything about the goal we've set for ourselves for this program?

Child-within, thank you very much for talking with me. I'd like to continue these conversations with you every day now and get to know you much better so we can learn to pull together at all times and both be more content. I promise to be more conscious of your presence moment by moment and I ask for your patience while I re-learn a few things for us.

Now immediately re-wind and listen to your tape with the following quiz before you. As you listen, tick the adjectives that seem to you to best describe the nature of this relationship between you and your emotional self, your child-within.

Open and frank	Difficult and strained
Willing to learn	Both sides unwilling
about each other	One side unwilling

Friendly   Unfriendly
Caring   Rushed

Is your now-self:
Critical
Judgemental
Over-Analytical
Lost
Impatient
Accepting
Understanding
Encouraging
Focussed
Patient
Other?

Is your child-within:
Cooperative
Eager
Spontaneous
Powerful
Suspicious
Resentful
Un-cooperative
Frightened
Angry
Powerless
Other?

Who seems to be in control — you or your child-within?

What do you think needs to happen to make this relationship better than it is?

Session 5
Befriending your child-within (1)
Background

Your ideal function is simply to **listen** and ask questions that help the child explore the current topic further. Just as a good listening partner would listen to you, never interrupt or make judgements or admonish you in any way, your job as the adult in this relationship is to simply allow the child the total freedom to speak her truth without fear of being 'scolded' by you. You want your child-within to open up to you with total honesty and she will never do this if you belittle her in any way.

For instance, your child-within might confide in you that 'I often secretly felt that I hated my family'. You might respond, 'That's not very nice'. 'Maybe not, but it's true!' will be your very next child-within thought. And the conversation within you will grind to a halt as a consequence of your moralising. The best thing to do then is apologise to your child-within and ask her to tell you more about hating the family. Only then will you begin to get to your inner negative truths — your limiting beliefs. You don't have to agree with your child-within's thoughts or feelings, but you do have to accept them as her truth. For you cannot change negativity until you know its precise nature. And this is your ultimate goal — to change your negative, or limiting, beliefs that lie under your child-within's negative thoughts and emotions.

Do not, under any circumstances, add insult to injury by mentally berating yourself because you notice how you continue to abuse or ignore yourself after you have decided not to — it is a lifetime habit, so go easy on yourself, give yourself a little time. Many people have found it helpful when noticing themselves still at it to say to themselves, to their child-selves, 'Sorry! There I go again! But at least I notice now!'

Aim

The purpose of the next two sessions is to practise relating to yourself, your child-within, in a more constructive way.

Instructions

The process is in two parts. A self-parenting conversation, followed by listening to the replay of the conversation on tape. Set up your two chairs, photograph, etc. as for previous self-parenting sessions. You will need your journal and the quiz you completed at the end of the last session, Session 4. Do not read any of this process on automatic pilot. Stop after each paragraph and convey its content to your child-within in your own words. The conversation should take at least twenty minutes. Switch on your tape recorder.

Process

Begin by explaining to your child-within that there is now time available for the two of you to spend together, why it is important that you do this, and what you are hoping to achieve by doing this. Then ask for her cooperation and give your assurance that you are serious about listening without interrupting or making judgements or admonishing in any way, that you want to allow her total freedom to speak her truth without being belittled or scolded by you.

Start to take responsibility for your child-within's needs by asking about them, chatting about them and responding to them as you think appropriate. The following questions are you now, speaking to your child-within:

So, child-within, how are you feeling right now?

How was your day? I'd like to hear all about how it went for you.

(E.g. What did you enjoy/not enjoy? Is there anything you want changed for tomorrow?)

Will you tell me about some of the favourite things you like to do of an evening?

(E.g. What are they? When did you last do them? Would you like to do them more often?)

Will you tell me about some of your all-time favourite books?

(E.g. What? What exactly was it you liked? How long since you read the last one?)

Let's chat about the way we usually spend our weekends.

(E.g. How? Like/dislike? Obstacles? Want more of? Ideal?)

Would you tell me about a time recently when you felt particularly happy?

Would you tell me about our friends?
(E.g. Who? Do we have enough? Close enough/too close? What do you like about each of them?)
Is there anything else you want to talk with me about right now?
Child-within, thank you very much for talking with me. I'd like to continue these conversations with you and get to know you much better so we can learn to pull together at all times and both be more content. I promise to be more conscious of your presence moment by moment and I ask for your patience while I re-learn a few things for us.

Re-wind your tape and listen to it with the aim of listening for any changes in the nature of your inner relationship since Session 4. Have the quiz from the end of Session 4 in front of you to help you. Note any changes in your journal.

Session 6
Befriending your child-within (2)
Background, Aim, Instructions

As for Session 5.

Process

Child-within, are you comfortable at the moment?
Is there anything you are wanting to discuss urgently with me?
Do you enjoy exercising? (E.g. What is your favourite form of exercise? When did you last do it? What exercise do you hate? Do you need more/less?)
Will you tell me about the people you most love? (E.g. Who? Why? When did you last tell them? Are you having problems with them at present? Do you need to contact anyone soon?)
Will you tell me about a time recently when you felt anxious?
Will you tell me about a time recently when you felt angry?
Let's chat about the best and worst parts of today.

What is the best thing that has happened to you recently?
Child-within, thank you very much for talking with me. I'd like to continue these conversations with you and get to know you much better so we can learn to pull together at all times and both be more content. I promise to be more conscious of your presence moment by moment and I ask for your patience while I re-learn a few things for us.

Re-wind your tape and listen to it with the aim of listening for any changes in the nature of your inner relationship since Session 4. Have the quiz from the end of Session 4 in front of you to help you. Note any changes in your journal.

Session 7
Retrieving your child-within
Background

A visualisation is not about inventing things. It is about allowing what is already there to come into fuller awareness. So do not try to script the sequence of images, just let them flow of their own making, as a dream does. This particular visualisation is a way of letting yourself know with your mind what you already know in your heart, and thus make it more real and more accessible for you to work with. It is also, conversely, a way of gaining non-rational understanding beyond that of which you may already be rationally aware.

Don't be worried if you find you are unable to actually 'see' the scenes in this or any other visualisation. Many people are not strongly 'visual', but process information kinaesthetically (that is, in an intuitive, feeling way) and it is easier and more effective for those people to simply have a sense of the situations.

Aim

The purpose of this visualisation is to put you into direct contact with the child you once were.

Instructions

Read through the visualisation first. If, having done this, you feel you would like to have another person on hand in case you need emotional support after doing the visualisation, be sure there is someone in the house with you to whom you can turn if necessary, before proceeding.

If you are aware that there was violence in your childhood, *do not replay any violence*. This includes incest, beatings or extreme physical or emotional deprivation. At the appropriate place during the visualisation, simply acknowledge in words to yourself, 'and then there was violence', and proceed to the section of the visualisation where the child-you runs to the adult-you standing at the door watching, and proceed from there.

This is a three-part process beginning with a Guided Visualisation. This is followed by a de-briefing segment and then an initial beliefs-clarifying exercise. It is important that you do all of this session at one time, so set aside an hour and a half to complete it fully. This does not include the time you may spend taping the visualisation in the first place.

The Guided Visualisation itself should take about ten minutes, with frequent pauses to give you time to respond within yourself. You can either tape this visualisation and play it back to yourself, or ask someone else to read it to you. Precede this visualisation with a five-minute relaxation time, which you could do by playing quiet music or beginning your tape with quiet music, if you do not already use another particular method.

Process

a) **The Visualisation**

Commence with five minutes' relaxation.

Now imagine yourself stepping into a long tunnel of light that carries you through the passage of time back to the past. See the years swish by you — last year (pause), ten years ago (pause), twenty years ago (pause) and so on back past the years to a scene from your childhood, a scene in which you are with other members of your family and things are not as you needed them to be.

See it as though you are standing unseen by the door, a visitor from the future, an invisible observer, unnoticed by anyone else, and just let the scene unfold, easily, as though it were an old movie. Perhaps there are several scenes. Perhaps just the one.

Look around this place. Notice its main features. What strikes you most about this place? See your parents, your brothers and sisters, and anyone else who was significant back then. What are they saying or doing?

And see yourself there too, a young child for whom things are not really the way she needs them to be. What is this child-you doing?

How are your parents responding? What are they saying or doing?

What are the others saying or doing to you?

What happens then? And now what's happening?

Watch it all get worse and worse. Notice how the tension mounts in the child-you.

What is she doing now?

What is she feeling? Perhaps she is bewildered and confused, or isolated and lonely, unable to reach her parents in the way she really needs to. Perhaps she is feeling harassed by her brothers or sisters — frustrated.

What is it she's feeling that she can't fully express? Is it how sad and lost she feels? Or how angry she is? Or is it anxiety and fear she is feeling?

What has she learnt to believe about herself in this family? Perhaps she's learnt to believe 'I don't really matter much' or 'I can't get what I need' or 'No-one's ever there for me'.

Does she feel that 'There's never enough for me' — enough love, or care, or time, or protection, or understanding? Or does she feel that 'There's too much' — overprotectiveness, or chaos, or emotion, or authoritarianism?

Notice how frightening it is to her to feel this way and not be able to really express it, and how much she needs to be heard openly and fully without fear of retribution, without fear of losing further love and approval.

As you stand there loving her and recognising her need to be heard, she turns and sees you. She recognises you as herself from the future, the one who's been making an effort lately to get to know her, and she runs to you for comfort.

Pick her up or take her hand and lead her gently from that place. It's OK with the others.

Take her out of that place and together slip effortlessly back into the tunnel of light, the passage of time. As you travel forward through the tunnel, she simply, easily, merges into you, into your heart, naturally becoming one with you.

And now it is safe for her to fully express herself without fear of adverse reaction, safe for her to unburden herself at last, knowing that you want to love her totally, unconditionally, exactly as she is — with all her troublesome feelings, all her limiting beliefs, all her child-like needs and all the difficult ways she acts when trying to get them met.

Allow yourself to just be in a space of unconditional, non-judgemental, self-acceptance.

(Long pause — as long as you need)

b) **Debriefing**
Either share your experience of that visualisation with your sharing partner, or go through and answer the questions below in writing. Either way, use the questions that follow.

1. Were you able to imagine a scene or scenes from your childhood where things were not as you needed them?	*Yes:* continue to 2. *No:* A 'no' is unusual — perhaps you were just too worried about actually 'seeing' the scenes and need to re-do it, allowing yourself to simply have a sense of the scenes. If this was not the

2. What was your child-within's main feeling in the unsatisfactory situation you were asked to recall?

3. What did your child-within most need more of?

4. What kinds of things do you think your child-within learnt to believe about herself and life in general in this situation?

5. Was your inner-child willing to come back to the present with you?

6. Did you experience a sense of oneness with her and acceptance of her?

problem, then we suggest you re-do Sessions 4, 5, 6, then try again.

If you answer 'yes' to questions 5 and 6, proceed to the clarifying exercise below.

If you answer 'no' to questions 5 or 6, it is probably because your child-within does not trust you enough yet. After all, you've ignored her for a long time, so that's understandable. You need to progress more slowly, to convince her you are really there for her and are not going away again. Spend more time doing self-parenting sessions similar to those in the previous sessions. You can simply put aside time each day, set up your two chairs and talk about whatever you want to with your child-within. Or you could buy one of the books recommended at the back of this book that has self-parenting exercises in it for you to do. If you persist with these exercises and the rest of the program, she will most certainly come around and begin opening up to you. You can then re-do this visualisation. For now, continue with the clarifying exercise that follows.

c) **Clarifying Exercise**

Following is a list of commonly held limiting beliefs. Mark any which you feel, at this moment, your child-within may have formed in the environment from which you have just taken her. This is a preliminary exploration, so just relax and trust your current feelings. Do it spontaneously rather than ponder over it, as your initial response will be much more accurate. Spend only a few minutes on it. There will be opportunities later to further clarify your limiting beliefs program.

I can't get what I most need, no matter how hard I try.
Others are never really there for me.
Others always let me down.
Others should be more caring.
Others are more important than I am.
I'm OK, but they're not.
I'd be happy if others were different.
It's never safe to relax.
I have to be strong.
I'm responsible for others/for it all.
I have to achieve to be valued.
I should put others first.
I'm not quick/clever/etc. enough.
I'm not as good as I should be.
No matter how hard I try, it's never good enough.
I'm responsible for others' problems.
I have to be bright and fun to be noticed.
Nothing matters.
Nothing I do makes any difference.
Life's boring and I'm powerless to change things.
I can't think straight.
I must be logical and rational, not intuitive or emotional.
All is lost and so am I.
I'll never be happy because now it is impossible.
I get attention only when I'm in trouble.

Feelings smother me.

I must not feel.

I am what I do.

I'm bad/no good/dirty/evil.

I should be seen and not heard.

I have to be the centre of attention.

You can't trust anyone.

Life is dull and boring without drama going on.

Life is difficult.

Life is a struggle.

Life is unfair.

Life happens to me.

Life is chaotic.

You can't expect much from life.

Life is worrying.

Life is hard.

Life is out of my control.

There is never enough.

I am not OK as I am.

I am not important.

My needs don't matter.

I am not lovable.

I have to be good and compliant.

I mustn't rock the boat.

I have to get it right.

It's not OK to make mistakes.

I am different.

I have to prove myself.

I have to struggle to get my needs met.

I am responsible when things go wrong.

I have to do it all.

I have to be the peacemaker.

I will never be good enough.

I have to be in control.

I don't have any control.

I have to be bright and cheery.

I must not question things.

I have to keep up appearances.

It's not OK to have fun.

No matter what I do it's not right.

Everything happens to me.

I am not capable.

I have to hide my feelings.

I have to please others.

Session 8
Becoming aware of your self-talk
Background

Earlier in the book we talked about the 'ABC' of Activating Events, Beliefs and Consequences (page 13). The idea is that when things happen to us — the 'activating events' of life — we often blame the event for our responses and reactions. However, different events lead to vastly different inner responses, or self-talk: remember the story of the friend who didn't show up and the possible responses. The event need not be momentous: it could be as simple as a remark that a person makes to you or a news item you see on television.

But what actually intervenes between the 'activating event' and the 'consequence' — the inner response — is a core belief.

Aim

The purpose of this exercise is to heighten your awareness of self-talk and limiting beliefs.

Instructions

Here are some examples of possible self-talk in three different situations. Read them through and notice which of these responses would be closest to yours.

Process

You are at a meeting at work and your colleague Helen, as always, makes many suggestions. Your possible self-talk goes:

I should back her up in this suggestion, but what will they think of me then?

I wish I was as smart as she is.

We've tried most of those before. Doesn't she remember?

It's obvious that won't work.

There she goes again. Blowing her own trumpet.

Who's she trying to impress now?

She deserves a promotion.

I can never get a word in edgeways.

She thinks she knows everything.

When is this meeting ever going to end?

Helen wears a lot of green. It suits her.

What's she on about?

You arrive home to find that your teenage son is sitting back watching television, not having done any jobs around the house. Your possible self-talk goes:

He's having a hard time at the moment. I'll let him be.

Lazy slob. He'll have to move out and look after himself.

Just like his father/mother. Irresponsible!

Typical eighteen-year-old! They drive me nuts.

He probably needs a bit of encouragement.

He's rebelling as usual. I'm not getting into a power game with him.

I'll leave it to his father/mother to handle it. I don't know what to do.

He could have done something! That's it! I'm not cooking dinner for him.

I think he needs help. Someone mentioned a good psychologist the other day.

He's probably wishing he was out with friends. Poor thing!

He's left it all to me as usual.

He's got too much on his plate. I'll do his jobs for him.

You and your partner/spouse, are driving somewhere for dinner and are running late. Neither of you knows the way to where you are going and your partner/spouse, who is driving, gets lost. Your possible self-talk goes:

I should have looked it up before we left home.

Why didn't you look it up before we left home?

I thought you knew how to get there.

You always do this.

Why do I have to take care of everything?

See! If I don't take control there's chaos.

Calm down! We'll get there eventually.

Why are we always in such a rush?

Why are things always so difficult?

What will our friends think when we are late?

Oh! Look at that interesting house over there.

This is fun! We're lost!

Now write down three situations you were in today and, for each situation, recall your self-talk. What other self-talk might you have had? Use the examples above as a guide.

Write down the names of some other people you know who have different personalities from yours and write down what you imagine their self-talk might be in those same situations from today.

Now think about some likely beliefs that might create such self-talk for the other people you have chosen.

Now look for some likely beliefs that might be creating your own self-talk.

Session 9
Tuning in to your self-talk
Background

As we saw in Part One, we develop our beliefs program not only through our interactions with our parents and immediate family, but also from the injunctions, spoken and unspoken, which we received from peer groups, guardians, society, the church — in fact all the individuals and groups of people we have known since we were born.

Aim

The purpose of the following exercise is to enable you to clarify beliefs you will have formed from this wider field of influence, including your family.

Instructions

Write down your immediate response; that is, your first thoughts straight off the top of your head, unedited in any way, to the following injunctions. To the injunction 'I'm too ...' one might respond, 'lazy, bossy, young, loud, untidy, outspoken, sensitive, etc., etc.' Or you may find that this particular injunction, 'I'm too...', triggers little or nothing for you, whereas you may respond easily when this injunction is presented as 'You're too'. That is, you may more easily hear other people's voices telling you how to be, rather than your own.

Process

I'm too ...
I have to be more ...
Nice people don't ...
I should ...
I shouldn't ...
I'm not ...
You're too ...

You should be more …
You should …
You shouldn't …
You're not …

Now consider the following beliefs to see if you can relate to any of them. Mark those you think you hold.

My decisions don't count.
I have to be right.
The only thing to trust/value is my own mind.
Emotions are dangerous.
Emotions are for women/men.
Emotions are to be avoided.
Emotions are childish.
Emotions are a sign of weakness.
Emotions just happen to me.
Emotions are stupid.
Emotions are uncontrollable.
What I feel is more important than anything else.
Women are relatively powerless without a man beside them.
Men are relatively powerless without a woman beside them.
Women/men are illogical.
Women/men are over-emotional.
Women/men have to struggle.
You can't trust women/men.
Women/men have to be nurturing and supportive.
Women/men have a hard life.
Women/men are passive victims.
Women/men are inferior.
Women are not as important as men.
Men are not as important as women.
Women/men take all the responsibility.
Women/men do all the work.
Women/men are always busy and in control.
Women are stronger than men.

Men are stronger than women.

Women/men should always look good.

Men are bastards.

Women/men have to be strong.

Women/men have to be successful.

Men have to protect women.

Women/men let me down.

Women/men are wimps.

Women/men are oppressors.

Women/men get the breaks.

It's a man's/woman's world.

Women/men are not there for me.

Women/men are weak.

Women/men don't know anything about love.

Women/men are boss.

Session 10
Compiling your limiting beliefs
Instructions

Looking at your lists of likely limiting beliefs from all the previous sessions, develop a complete list for yourself of what you now consider to be your own limiting beliefs — your limiting beliefs program. This might involve eliminating any repetition in the lists you have so far compiled.

Session 11
Exploring your limiting beliefs
Aim

The purpose of these next sessions is for you to explore your limiting beliefs with your child-within, and finally to choose those you want to change first.

Instructions

For this session you will need your complete list from the previous session. You will be talking with your child-within about these beliefs, so set up your two chairs etc. as for previous self-parenting sessions. You can tape this session and then if you get stuck anywhere in the process, replay the tape. Listening to yourself will probably help.

Proceed through the beliefs from your list, one by one, in the way outlined below, until your half-hour or so is up. Don't try to cover them all, as you can repeat this session until you do get through them all. Just concentrate on a few at a time, and don't rush through them. You can repeat this session as many times as you need to in order to cover all of the beliefs you have clarified.

Process

Hello child-within. How is your body feeling right now? Tense? Exactly where? Like to relax it? Need a stretch? A drink? Anything else?

Let's talk about these beliefs of ours now. (Begin with the first belief on your list.) Is this quite it? Or is it something slightly different? Where did you get it from? How does it feel? What effect does it have on our life now? On our life in the past? Would you like to be rid of it? Let's explore how it would be for us if we were rid of it.

Write down the precise belief you have now clarified with your child-within.

Repeat, working your way through your list until your time is up.

Child-within, thank you for helping me to understand you more clearly.

Repeat this session as many times as you need to until you have covered your entire list.

Final session
Core and branch beliefs
Background

Re-read the section on core and branch beliefs on page 30. From the previous exercises you will have developed a sense of how some of your beliefs are variations on others, and of how some are variations on one theme. For example, 'Life is chaotic', together with 'Things always go wrong for me', together with 'Emotions are uncontrollable' could all be branches of a core belief, 'I'm powerless'. Or 'I have to work hard to be accepted', together with 'I have to be needed by others to be valued', together with 'I must always look attractive to be acceptable' could all be branches of a core belief, 'I'm not OK as I am'.

Aim

The purpose of this exercise is to single out your core limiting beliefs.

Instructions and Process

Using the model of the tree, see if you can distinguish between your branch and core beliefs. Don't be concerned if this is not all instantly obvious to you. You will find that it becomes clearer as you live with your increasing awareness of your beliefs.

When you have clarified some of your core limiting beliefs, choose one or two that you feel are presently most limiting to you, or causing you most difficulty and struggle.

Clarifying your limiting beliefs in future

Now that you have established a working, accepting relationship with your inner-child, you will not have to repeat all of this work on clarifying your limiting beliefs again. From now on throughout the rest of your life, whenever you feel a negative emotion or catch yourself thinking negatively, you can tune in and allow your inner-child to freely and fully express all about that particular negative emotion or thought. Your job will be to listen without judgement and with total self-acceptance. You will need to ask questions that encourage your inner-child to tell you all there is to be said about these particular feelings, while you listen carefully for the limiting belief hidden in her words.

You are now ready to move on to the final section of the book — 'Changing Your Limiting Beliefs'.

PART FOUR

Changing Your Limiting Beliefs

Now for the best news — your reward for having met the challenge of going with your negative thoughts and feelings instead of trying to flee from them. Changing your limiting beliefs is relatively straightforward. Just think — if in response to your early environment you programmed yourself so powerfully with beliefs before you had the assistance of adult assessment and reasoning, how much more powerfully are you able to re-program yourself now that you have at your disposal not only a child's insight, intuition and emotional energy, but also the discernment and logic of your adult mind.

Your attitude matters

You will need your adult faculties switched on to understand that since your limiting beliefs have been powerfully running you for many years now, they have gathered much energy and momentum. It is as though you are sitting in the back seat of a powerful, speeding car with a mind of its own; one that is relentlessly taking you where it will as you sit, formerly unaware perhaps, that you were even in it. But now that you have clarified and understood the power of your limiting beliefs, it is as though you are more and more frequently aware of where you are placed and increasingly wanting to stop the car, take over the controls, place your hands firmly on the steering wheel and drive to where you want to be. To achieve this takeover, you are going to have to do three things:

Learn how to stop the car.

Exert a physical effort to climb into the driver's seat.

Apply your knowledge.

It is necessary that you actively engage in each step of the process.

We cannot deny that occasionally people step straight out of a belief on simply recognising it — but that usually occurs when the person has had lots of experience of changing her beliefs, or when the belief has been so demonstrably false as to appear totally ludicrous as soon as it is exposed. But in perhaps 95 per cent of cases the change process is exactly that — a process.

The process of changing your beliefs is straight-forward, but requires a sustained effort.

It is simply not realistic to expect to change limiting beliefs without exerting sustained effort. It isn't that the process is difficult, it just requires your full engagement. For such a commitment to yourself and the quality of the rest of your life, you will be abundantly rewarded. The time it will take you to change any one limiting belief will be determined largely by the level of your engagement in the process of change.

There can be other reasons why a belief takes longer to move. You may recall Emma (in Part Two) who had to structure a particular program for herself to move through the beliefs that kept her from being focussed and reliable, or Dan who had to begin with body-work therapy before he could commence working directly on his beliefs. Emma and Dan represent two distinct belief systems which can require longer work. Throughout the book we recommend additional approaches that may be necessary in individual situations. Chief among these is the situation where one's childhood was so traumatic that longer-term private therapy is recommended in addition to beliefs change work, or the situation where one finds oneself in frequent emotional overwhelm, either as the result of such a childhood or as the result of recent trauma like the death of a loved one, or a recent divorce.

The process of changing beliefs

We mentioned the major approaches to changing beliefs in our case studies, namely self-parenting conversations, affirmations and energy work, and we will cover each of these approaches here. However, there are certain fundamentals which must be thoroughly understood, and borne in mind throughout any and all change work. We have touched on them already in this book, but consider them so fundamentally important that we want to repeat them here.

First, in our experience, it is simply not possible to effect permanent inner change in your head alone, for your beliefs are held as much in your emotions, your energy system and your body as they are held in your head. It is no use trying to permanently change your limiting beliefs as a purely intellectual exercise.

In the field of personal change we must move forward on two feet – intellect and experience, head and heart, reason and emotions.

To be effective, personal change must occur in your head and your heart. This means that the change work must be done in experiential contact with your child-within, who is your emotions and your past, just as the clarifying work was done. Your change work must also involve physical energy, since tied up with each limiting belief are emotions, which manifest themselves in physical energy. This energy simply must be re-directed. We have only to look at the way others hold themselves — their bodies — to realise that personality — their beliefs — is embedded in our very musculature. Similarly, if we observe the way different people with different personalities move or carry themselves, it is clear that their beliefs about life and themselves are also embedded in their energy systems. If you would like to learn more about these insights, the bibliography suggests several books of interest.

The work of reprogramming must always be undertaken with a loving attitude towards yourself, for it involves switching your inner conversations from ridicule and contempt whenever you find yourself acting out of the old program, to understanding, acceptance and re-education instead. Whenever you notice yourself acting or re-acting out of an old, limiting belief, it is death to any attempts to change if you respond with self-criticism and do not correct this as soon as you notice you have done it. We will give you guidelines for doing this below.

Finally, it is important that you work on one belief at a time.

Step 1
Belief vs reality

Be clear about the precise belief you want to be rid of. Consider how you came to hold this belief. Be clear about its origins as the child-you's response to your childhood environment. What would you say to a friend who gave you those same reasons for such a belief? Be clear in your mind that this was the result of your childhood perception of reality, and not reality. Be clear therefore that this belief is not true, is a misunderstanding of reality, and is in fact preposterous nonsense. You may want to talk this through with a friend to achieve this level of intellectual insight. If not, write down the story of 'How I got this belief and why it is not reality'.

Step 2
Guided visualisation
Purpose and value

When one is trying to learn a new skill, or a new way of looking at something, experience is a powerful teacher. If one is trying to learn to drive a car (to continue our analogy at the beginning of Part Four) one can talk about it, read about it, be told about it, and that helps. But until one actually begins to do it, the knowledge remains un-usable, static.

In some aspects, the human mind does not distinguish between an imagined event and an actual event. The same physiological reactions occur in our bodies whether we are watching a scary movie or in a scary situation ourselves: the same emotional responses occur. So imagining an event is a very powerful way to prepare for an event, as many sporting champions know. Trials have been done on the power of visualisation in the sporting arena and we know that a team that spends time imagining winning as well as practising is more likely to actually win than a comparable team that practises only.

Creative visualisation is therefore a highly effective way to learn — and we are talking about effective learning that is not only retained, but is easily translated into action. All you have to do is participate fully, really allow yourself to be in the situation and allow yourself to experience what it feels like. The visualisation is constructed so as to appeal to all your major senses, which maximises its effectiveness.

Preparation

First, briefly read through this visualisation. If, having done this, you feel you would like to have another person on hand in case you need emotional support after doing the visualisation, be sure there is someone in the house with you to whom you can turn, if necessary, before proceeding.

As for the visualisation in Part Three, you can ask a friend to read this one to you or you can put it on tape; or you may prefer to read it as you go, closing your eyes to do each bit.

Set up your environment so that you will not be disturbed in any way whatsoever and so you are comfortable. Do not lie down, as you may tend to fall asleep. Have the book close by.

Now, using the same limiting belief you have been working with in Steps 1 and 2, decide on a belief you want to have in its place. These are the two beliefs you will use in the visualisation — an old limiting belief and a new positive belief.

You will be relaxing and then proceeding through this process slowly, taking all the time you need to achieve clarity. If it is difficult for you to see pictures in your mind, just allow yourself to have a sense of the situation, in whatever way works for you.

The actual visualisation should move along at a pace that is comfortable for you, but do not get bogged down; keep it moving as it would if you were in a group and the leader was reading the visualisation to you at a steady pace. If you find a particular aspect difficult to visualise or feel a sense of, just move on.

The visualisation

Relax in whatever way you prefer, for five minutes or more (if you are a meditator, do a full meditation).

Now, as though you were sitting in a cinema watching a movie on a large screen, see yourself on that screen going through life from the present time forward, with this old belief intact. Make a graphic picture or have a powerful sense of yourself as the end product of this belief alone. See what it is costing you:

In your relationships. (Pause)

Mentally.   (Pause)

Emotionally.   (Pause)

Financially.   (Pause)

Physically.   (Pause)

Spiritually.   (Pause)

As the movie runs on, have a picture of the total pain of holding onto this belief — a picture or a sense of yourself as the end product of this belief alone. (Pause)

Now make it all as bad as you can bear. What is the worst that could happen if you keep this belief? (Pause)

Now ask yourself for how much longer you want to keep this belief.

Watch the movie run backwards very quickly to the present time, see the scenes going backwards, feel your feelings returning to what they were, hear any sounds backwards. Faster and faster it runs backwards. (Pause)

Now, what is your chosen new belief, the belief with which you would like to replace this old limiting belief? (Pause)

As though watching a movie, see yourself going through life from the present time forward, with this new belief. Make a graphic picture, or have a powerful sense of yourself as the end product of this belief alone. See what it gains you:

In your relationships. (Pause)

Mentally. (Pause)

Emotionally. (Pause)

Financially. (Pause)

Physically. (Pause)

Spiritually. (Pause)

As the movie runs on, have a picture of the total joy of holding onto this belief — a picture or a sense of yourself as the end product of this belief alone. (Pause)

Now have a sense of stepping into the movie and being this picture of yourself. (Pause)

Give it an image — what does it look like, having this new belief? Whatever image springs to mind. (Pause)

Give it a sound — what sound do you associate with this belief? Whatever sound springs to mind. (Pause)

Give it a feeling — what feeling do you associate with this belief? Whatever feeling springs to mind. (Pause)

Go back to the visual image you had for this belief and make it bigger, make it brighter, make it clearer and closer. Make it as big and as bright, as clear and as close as you like. (Pause)

Go back to the sound and turn it up, so that it is as loud as you'd like it to be; an exquisite tone, beautifully balanced. (Pause)

Go to the feeling and exaggerate it to its fullest expression. How does it feel now? (Pause)

Step out of the movie into here and now.

Step 3
Imaging

Take the final image of yourself from the guided visualisation, the image of yourself with your new belief in place, and use it frequently for the next week. At a minimum, recall it three times a day — link it to daily activities so you don't forget it — showering, dressing, eating, waking, going to bed.

You can proceed to Step 4 as soon as you wish — it is not intended that you wait out the week.

Step 4
Good self-parenting
The concept again

As we have explained earlier, our need for nurturing care, for good parenting in other words, does not stop when we turn eighteen or twenty-one or even fifty-one. It remains a basic human need and as such is not something to be embarrassed about but rather something to freely admit exists within you. We have seen in our case studies how easy it is for us to deny our own needs for nurture, as Gordon and Carol did, or to make that need the responsibility of other people, as Kerry did. We also saw how some of us remain essentially children, as Emma had, and have not learnt to set boundaries and stick to our goals so that we can function in the adult world effectively — we do not provide for ourselves the 'discipline' and structure that a good parent would. These are the major ways in which we can fail to be a good parent to ourselves.

To change our beliefs it is necessary that we learn to parent ourselves effectively. There are many books available on this topic, and it would be a good idea to read one in the near future; we recommend several at the back of this book. But from the work you have already done to clarify your limiting beliefs, you should now have an idea of and feel for what constitutes good self-parenting. It is the same as what constitutes good external parenting.

To permanently change our beliefs it is also essential that we work with our emotional history in an experiential way. Your inner-child is the perfect vehicle for such work.

Listen to your child-within with unconditional acceptance. Stop judging her. Start understanding why she is the way she is and simply accept and love her. Remember, acceptance does not mean you don't want to change the way she feels or what she has come to believe. The way to do that is to understand what is and has been and work with it. Like any child, your child-within will feel better and cooperate more fully when you stop nagging her and start listening to her side of things, or when you stop absenting yourself and learn to be there for her, lovingly setting a stabilising structure in place for her. It is all in the way you talk to yourself.

Our attachment to our limiting beliefs

Even though our limiting beliefs cause us pain and struggle, we are often deeply attached to a particular belief. Although this has been discussed in Part One, it is important enough to be repeated here. We took on most of our limiting beliefs originally as a way of adapting to our childhood environment, and we did this because we considered these beliefs to be the very best way to make sense of, and indeed survive, our environment. So our child-within may take a little convincing that a particular belief is no longer necessary for survival.

Also, we can be attached to a particular belief because there is often a pay-off to holding onto the belief. In a self-destructive way, we do derive a 'benefit' from it. If I hold a belief that 'Life happens to me and I am powerless' then I get to be 'Not responsible' for whatever happens to me. If I hold a belief that 'I have to get everything right' and I have spent my life ensuring that I usually do, then I probably get to feel superior to most other people because they appear to 'Get things wrong' a lot of the time.

Another reason for not wanting to let go of a limiting belief is sometimes that our child-within does not feel it is safe to let go of that belief. Again, if I hold the belief that 'I am not powerful' then I may have built up an armoury of branch beliefs about power, such as 'Power is dangerous', 'Powerful people are not good people'. Indeed, like Lisa (page 52), when I was a child such may have been my very experience of 'power', or what I then perceived to be 'power'.

It is quite common for the child-within to be afraid to let go of the old belief, to feel that it is not safe to do so. After all, she has clung to it for this long for the very good reason that it made sense of things once, however painfully. Your job then is to reassure her that it is now safe and desirable to let go of it, to convince her it really is safe by explaining how you are going to make it safe by your unconditional acceptance and love.

Your task in your self-parenting conversations with your inner-child is to:

Find out what she needs.

Take responsibility for getting those needs met.

Respond to her fears about letting go of old limiting beliefs.

Lovingly set limits if she's running wild.

Instructions

Now is the time to check whether your child-within is ready to let go of the particular belief you are working on. You can do this by having a talk with your child-within about any such obstacles. Proceed as before by setting up two chairs facing each other. Sit in one chair and with your child-within in the other chair, explore the following topics. Use the photo of yourself as a child from Part Three, and remember to move back and forth between the chairs. Put on some very calming music; something slow. The adagio movements from baroque music are good.

Preliminary self-parenting session

Explore with your child-within what the both of you think and feel about undertaking this change work, and when you have come to a natural conclusion to the conversation, make the following solemn promise to your child-within.

'I promise to see this program through and to do whatever it takes to effect the changes we both want. I fully accept that I am responsible for this process and for meeting your unmet needs. I intend to be a good parent to you. I really do understand why you are the way you are, and I love and accept you unconditionally. I need you to understand that I am entering a sharp learning curve now and I will probably make mistakes sometimes. I need you to be patient while I re-learn some things for us because I promise I will be doing my best. It may not be perfect, but it will be my best, and I will learn as fast as I can. When I "blow it" by being critical or in any way judgemental of you, I will apologise as soon as I realise what I have done. Is this OK with you?'

Now listen to whatever your child-within has to say, respond, and continue back and forth until the conversation comes to a satisfactory resting place.

Talk with your child-within about the specific limiting belief you are working to change. Place your focus on listening to and re-educating your child-within.

Explain that you understand how this belief came about (elaborate fully).

Then explain that it is a belief, not reality; it is just a belief, not the truth. Explain that it is a belief she took on in an attempt to make sense of things at the time and/or to maintain parental attention and approval. Talk about the details of how this occurred.

Follow this by reassuring your child-within that the truth is something quite different and that you will give her attention and approval regardless of this belief. (For example, if the belief is 'I have to be constantly busy' you might reassure your child-within that this is no longer true — that you will give her permission to relax when need be, and approval for actually relaxing.)

Listen and respond to whatever your inner-child has to say about this. Be sure you have acknowledged the original importance of the belief.

If you are an 'Emma-type' personality (that is, if your inner-child is accustomed to calling the shots and needs to be reined in with some self-discipline and structure) explain this now. Explain why she will be better off — why she will feel better for it as you start to achieve goals and be reliable, etc. (You have probably already convinced her of this with the Guided Visualisation.)

Listen and respond. Listen and respond. Listen and respond.

Discuss the pay-offs or benefits you derive from holding onto this belief. Both of you must decide if you want to let go of these pay-offs. You will be able to completely let go of the old belief only when you are fully convinced about letting go of its pay-offs.

Discuss any fears your child-within might have about letting go of this particular belief. (Do not lecture about these fears being unrealistic. Rather hear, accept, and reassure and re-educate. Love your child-within out of her fears, rather than lecture her about them).

'Child-within, are you ready to go on with the change work?'

If the answer to this question is a resounding 'yes' then thank your child-within for cooperating and proceed to Step 5. However, if the answer to this question is in doubt, or is in fact 'no', you have two options.

You can continue to talk with your child-within over the next few days about her reservations, in the hope that by your listening carefully and your reassurance, the fears will soon subside. Re-read the section on page 118 about the concepts involved in good parenting.

Or you can choose another limiting belief to work on first and begin again with this belief at Step 1 of the change program. By changing a less emotionally charged belief first, you will probably demonstrate to your child-within that the process is safe and so be able to continue work on your initial limiting belief.

Step 5
Self-parenting on the go

From now on, foster your ability to notice yourself acting out of your old belief and react kindly to yourself. For example, whenever you hear yourself thinking critical or judgemental thoughts about yourself, or as you do your change work, or you catch yourself thinking thoughts like 'Damn it! There I go again! Same old program, different day. When will I ever learn?', stop in your tracks and apologise to your child-within. Say something like 'Ooops! Sorry! I'm abusing you again! But at least I am noticing when I do that now, so we are progressing. And I promise to keep working to change things for us'.

This is essential and it is the point that most people have to be reminded of constantly until it becomes second nature. So write a few reminder notes to yourself right now and put them where you will see them for the next few days, or until you take this attitude on board. Failure to assimilate this patient attitude towards yourself will undermine your entire change program.

Step 6
Understanding and using affirmations
Meaningless jingle or powerful tool for change?

Let's say it right up-front — there's been a lot of hype and nonsense over the past decade about the use of affirmations. 'Every day in every way I'm becoming better and better' just won't pass muster any more. But let's not throw out the baby with the bathwater, because when correctly used affirmations are an extremely powerful tool. The question is, what constitutes 'correct use'?

First, using an affirmation to try to change a negative-thought pattern without having clarified the belief that is causing the negative thinking, is merely practising positive thinking, and as mentioned in Part One this does not usually take permanent hold. Using an affirmation to try to change a negative emotional state without clarifying the belief that is causing the emotions, is practising emotional denial and therefore fundamentally undermines the change process.

To be powerfully effective, we believe affirmations are best used at the beliefs level, which is the core level of our personalities. Then we are not denying anything or trying to stick a band-aid over anything — we have accepted the core truth within ourselves that is causing our pain and struggle, and we are working to heal ourselves at that core level.

To be effective, we also believe that an affirmation must be individually tailored. It must be directed at your limiting belief, in language which speaks to you.

Writing your own personal affirmations

1. Write down the belief you wish to change.

2. Write a statement that is its opposite and which is:

Positive (no negative qualities, no not's or no's).

Personal (use your name or the pronoun 'I').

Concise (one issue at a time; not too complex a sentence).

Present tense (as though you have this quality now).

For example, Belief to be changed: 'I always have to please others'. Affirmation: 'I (personal) now bravely do (present) what is right for me, and others' reactions are their responsibility' (positive and concise).

You can also use an affirmation to address an unmet need. Your limiting belief may indeed be about not getting your needs met.

For example, Situation or belief: 'My parents pay no attention to me'. Affirmation: 'I get lots of attention from myself, and I am surrounding myself with caring and attentive others' (that is, I take responsibility for my need for attention and accept my parents as they are).

The process of writing an affirmation that is just right for you takes a little time and thought. The aim is to come up with a statement to which you have a gut response of 'Yes! Yes! Yes! That's exactly what I want!' Someone else with exactly the same limiting belief as yours have may not respond to the same wording that you do. It has to be personally tailored to elicit this 'Yes! That's exactly it!' response within you.

So it will be a process of starting out with your limiting belief, writing down the first thing that comes into your head as a counter-statement to that belief, and honing it till it fits. Let's look at how this process evolved for Brett.

Brett had an over-protective mother and from experience he learnt that 'I can't do anything by myself'. The first statement he jotted down was 'I can do it all by myself'. But that didn't feel right to him, because he didn't want to do it all by himself. He was at a loss until he began to think around the limiting belief statement 'I can't do anything by myself'. When he questioned how else he might write this belief, and what other words came to mind when he considered this belief, he wrote down: 'I'm not capable. I'm not independent. I'm not successful. I'm not confident in my abilities'.

Then he had more to work with and began fashioning a statement that turned these negatives into positives. So he had 'I am capable, independent, successful and confident in my own abilities'.

He began playing with incorporating these qualities into a sentence that was just right for him. The sentence became 'I am confident that I am independently capable of success'. Now he felt he was getting somewhere, but he still had a vague feeling of unease about it, a feeling that it was not quite complete.

When he focussed on this feeling, and tried to put words to it, he heard a tiny voice inside himself saying, 'Great! That means I don't have to exert any effort; it'll all just happen'. Brett knew he was prone to lethargy and lack of motivation, and realised that he could interpret this sentence as it stood, to fuel his lack of motivation. So he added, 'Whenever I choose to apply myself'. The completed affirmation was 'Whenever I choose to apply myself I am confident that I am independently capable of success'. His eyes lit up and his whole mind and body said, 'Yes! That's what I need to know'.

Let's examine another attempt to construct the right affirmation. Zoe had been sent off to boarding school at five and at forty-five still felt frightened and alone. Her belief was 'I can't take care of myself'. So she quickly constructed an affirmation that read, 'I can take care of my own needs'. After using this affirmation for two days, she was a nervous wreck and had to take the day off work because she had been awake all night, crying, alone, terrified. Her affirmation was making her child-within feel worse, not better, so it was obviously not right for her.

Zoe's attempts highlight a common misunderstanding about what it means to take care of one's own needs. It does not mean that one is an island, capable of living without others. After all, one of our basic needs as human beings is for intimate relationships and social friendships. So taking care of one's own needs means that one takes care of these needs too. When this was explained to Zoe, she reworked her affirmation to read, 'I lovingly accept all my needs and do whatever it takes to meet them'. The subtle shift in emphasis that the rewording provided no longer sounded threatening to her and was now an acceptable starting point.

Some suggestions for affirmations to re-program common limiting beliefs

What follows are suggestions only. Please use them as starting points from which to develop your own affirmations.

I'm only acceptable if I'm busy.

I accept myself unconditionally and I honour my need to relax.
or I accept myself especially when I am simply being.
or It's safe for me to relax whenever I need to.

I have to get it right or I'm a failure.

It is safe for me to make mistakes — they are always opportunities to learn and grow.
or I accept myself, especially when I make mistakes.
or Mistakes are human and so am I.
or I am an acceptable and effective human being, even when I make mistakes.

All I have to do to win attention and approval is be bright and fun to be around.

I now focus on tasks and complete them on time.
or For my own greater fulfilment I now choose to be organised and reliable.
or It is safe for me to sit in silence and let others set the pace socially. I am a good listener.

It is not OK to feel my feelings. Feelings are not important / not acceptable / childish etc.

I accept all my feelings unconditionally.
or It is now safe/healthy/OK/ for me to feel all my feelings.
or I now accept my anger/sadness/fear and I learn from it/them.

Emotions are a sign of weakness / childish / for women only / dangerous.

I value and respect my emotions. It is healthy and safe to feel my feelings.

No matter how hard I try, it's never good enough.

I do my best and acknowledge myself for that. I accept myself unconditionally.

Being strong means rising above my emotions.

My strength is my ability to protect myself and get my needs met.
or My feelings matter. I matter.
or I listen to my own needs and feelings and act on them appropriately.

Anger is completely unacceptable.

I now accept my anger and I manage it appropriately.
or It is now safe for me to feel my anger and to communicate my needs.
or It is safe and necessary for me to be appropriately assertive.
or I flow with my anger and take care of the fears beneath it.
or I love my anger. It is a message that I listen to.

Nice people don't get angry / I never feel angry.

Real people feel and express their anger and I am real.
or When I am angry I say so, cleanly and clearly.
or I sometimes feel angry and that's good.

Other people cause my anger and it's OK to dump it on them.

My anger is my response and I communicate my needs appropriately.
or I manage the energy of my anger appropriately.

Life's confusing / I'm confused / It's all too complicated.

I calmly listen to my own needs and feelings and am guided by them.

My needs don't matter / I don't matter / I'm not important.

My needs matter / I matter.

Others' needs are more important than mine.

My needs are my first responsibility.
or My needs are as important as everyone else's.

Life happens to me / Others determine the outcomes in my life.

I accept responsibility for my own life.
or My beliefs, words and actions determine my outcomes in life; I am in charge of my own life.
or I am capable of getting my needs met and I make my choices accordingly.

I have to be in control of everything.	It is safe to let go. I allow others to be strong. **or** I quietly do what is right for me and allow others to control their own outcomes.
I am responsible for everything.	I am responsible for myself. **or** Others are capable of looking after themselves. **or** I allow others to assume responsibility for their own lives and to make their own mistakes. **or** When others make mistakes it is OK. I am innocent and free.
To be loved and appreciated I must achieve.	I love and appreciate myself for who I am regardless of what I achieve. **or** I accept myself unconditionally. **or** Being, listening and caring are as important as achieving.
If I let anyone too close, they'll take me over.	It is safe to be intimate with loved ones. **or** I am in full possession of myself and add to my being when I allow others close.
If I fit in with others they should be there for me.	Others are there for me when I am there for me. **or** When I am true to myself others can see who I am and be there for me.

or When I am true to myself I attract others who love and respect who I am.

Life's a struggle.	Life is as I make it. or My responses to life are up to me. or I respond to life's challenges with ease and vigour.
I can't get what I need no matter how hard I try.	I am capable of appropriate action to get what I need. or I am responsible for my own needs and I am guided by them.
To be lovable I must …	I am lovable just as I am. or When I am true to myself others love me for who I am.
*Other people should …	Others are / I am free to act as they / I see fit. or I release others to be different from me. or It is OK for me to be different.
*Others are out to get me / I can't trust anyone.	I trust myself and treat myself gently.
*Others ruin my life. Others are to blame.	I am blame-free and so are others. or I forgive myself and others. or I am responsible for creating my life as I want it.

| | **or** Others are as they are and I am responsible for my own life. **or** I take responsibility for my needs by surrounding myself with people who respect me as I respect myself. |

*Men/women are ...

Men/women are ... (the opposite). **or** I attract relationships with men/women who are ... (the opposite). **or** My inner male/female aspect is ... (the opposite).

Men have to be strong always.

Men are / I am free to feel my feelings and communicate them. **or** It's OK for me/men to need support.

*You can't trust men/women.

It is now safe for me to trust men/women. **or** I trust my own male/female aspect.

There is something terribly wrong with me.

I am absolutely OK just as I am. **or** I love and accept myself as I am.

The best way to handle conflict is to ignore it.

Conflict is a natural part of life. I accept it and look for what I can learn from it. **or** I now manage conflicts openly.

Conflict is a sign of moral weakness.	Conflict is part of nature. There is no such thing as a problem without a gift in its hands.
Personal problems are a sign of personal deficiency.	Personal problems are a chance to learn and grow.
I must stay safe and not take risks.	I am safe and I am free to take calculated risks. **or** Life is full of change and I welcome it. **or** Change makes life fun. **or** I enjoy change.
I shouldn't blow my own trumpet.	I freely and openly share my joys and successes.
*Others don't respect me enough.	I respect myself completely and I act in ways that are respectful to others.
I have to be one with someone else to be whole.	I am perfectly formed and whole within myself. †

† If you have this particular belief, this affirmation should be used as a gentle, loving reassurance to your child-within, not a denial of her reality, which may be a profound sense of something missing. You may need some personal therapy sessions to help you heal the emptiness within you. You might have the sense of a 'black hole' inside you, which is quite common, and often requires some sensitive and skilful therapy. Again, the way out lies in going with the emptiness, not trying to deny it by lighting it up or filling it artificially, which some therapies try to do. Work with a therapist who will honour what your child-within feels, not deny it. There are various approaches that can be very effective here.

The beliefs marked * are classic cases of projection, where we project our own fears onto others. Because fear is the last thing we ever want to feel, we have invented, clever creatures that we are, a cunning way to avoid it at all costs. At a deep, subconscious level we convince ourselves very early in life that the thing we fear (in this case our own fearful limiting belief) is in fact not inside us at all, but decidedly outside us. So it is, for instance, not me who doesn't trust myself, which is a fearful thought, but everyone else, or specific other people, who do not trust me, or whom I cannot trust.

The answer is to take back the projection and form an affirmation that gets to the heart of the matter, namely that we give ourselves whatever it is we are seeing in others. Remember, our beliefs determine the way we see others, and become self-fulfilling prophecies.

Using affirmations

Affirmations should be written up in as many places as possible and repeated frequently. The idea is to bombard yourself with the new belief for a period of time.

Buy a roll of large stick-on labels and write your affirmation on at least six of them. Now put up your affirmation in places where you will see it often. Some suggestions are:

the steering wheel of your car
behind the toilet door
over the vanity in the bathroom
by your telephone
on your computer
near where you make your tea or coffee, or some other prominent
    place in the kitchen
on the inside flap of your handbag if you use one
on your desk
on your bedside table.

If you are worried about being teased by others, write your affirmation in a way they will not understand — use another language or shorthand, write only the first letters of key words, or draw an image that will remind you to say the affirmation to yourself; you will know it off by heart very quickly anyway. One thing is certain. Affirmations do not work if you do not use them! You can make a mental movie of your affirmation, a picture of how things will be when this is your reality, and run this picture in your mind as well as saying the words. Mental images are more powerful for some people than words. Try both. Often.

Another idea, if you feel comfortable with it, is to enlist the support of people close to you. Ask them to say your affirmation to you several times a day, as Allan did with his wife and Gina did with her friends.

How do you know when to stop? When you find yourself saying the affirmation and thinking, 'I know that!' You know when you no longer need to use it because you simply no longer need whatever it is you are telling yourself — you have it. This could be after a week, or after several months. It all depends on so many different factors that there can be no right or wrong timing. However, if you are sure it is right for you, if you use it frequently and you combine it with the other change techniques suggested here, then a couple of months would probably be maximum. Refer also to the section on when to get help on pages 11, 132 and 140.

The dynamics of affirmations

Affirmations are not static things. On the contrary, they are extremely dynamic. As you use your affirmation it may drop to another level — that is, you may start to realise that there is more to this issue than had occurred to you, and so need to clarify the deeper layer and adjust your affirmation accordingly. Let's say you have a belief that 'Things always go wrong for me' and you've constructed an affirmation that says, 'Life now goes smoothly for me'. You might sail along with this affirmation for a time, then begin to feel you are not really getting to the core of the matter, so you sit with this feeling, thinking about it now and again, until it becomes clearer to you. In fact, what is likely to have happened is that suddenly things go even less smoothly for you than before. Affirmations are like that — they can force us to focus more closely on the problem by drawing our attention to just how bad the problem has become. This is your cue to look more closely, not to abandon ship. 'When in deep water, become a diver' (*The Book of Runes*, Angus & Robertson, 1984).

The deeper level will be that you have not got to the core belief, but are operating on a branch belief. The core belief, you realise as you continue to use your first affirmation, is 'I'm powerless'. So you would then re-work your affirmation. It might now read, 'I am capable of effecting my own outcomes in life and things go smoothly for me'.

So off you go, using this affirmation. Then you realise that you don't know how to effect your own outcomes in life — it's a totally new concept to you. So you mull over this for a while, maybe talk with friends, perhaps re-read sections of this book, and you realise what you need to begin doing is to take yourself more seriously — giving more credence to your own thoughts and opinions and feelings, so that you can effect your own outcomes. What you thought was the core belief, 'I'm powerless', actually holds another belief deep within it — the belief that 'I don't matter much'.

Now you're really making progress. You construct another affirmation that says: 'My needs, feelings and opinions matter. I matter'. You will now most certainly experience a marvellous sense of clarity, that enlivening 'Aha! That's it!', together with the excitement of knowing that you are on the home stretch. It won't be long now till you experience the sheer elation of change, deep within your body, mind and heart: not a cold intellectual grasp on a new concept, but a surge of long-blocked energy somewhere deep in your solar plexus. This is change at a 'gut' level. Congratulations! You're free! You've done it! And as your core belief tumbles, the branch beliefs will come tumbling down with it. You will have toppled the entire structure.

Jason was a young computer salesman who had a belief that he was stupid, to use his own word. As part of his change work, he began using an affirmation that 'I am intelligent and capable'. A week later he reported in amazement: 'I am absolutely stunned — it's as though my negative self-talk which has always been there and I've never noticed, is suddenly being broadcast through a loudspeaker. I'd be about to make a phone call at work and I'd hear in full stereo at top volume, "You won't be able to do it, dummy!", or I'd be talking to the boss about an idea I had and the loudspeaker in my head would boom, 'That's a stupid idea!' I began using my new affirmation on Saturday, and this loudspeaker effect operated on Monday, Tuesday, Wednesday. Each time, I couldn't believe my ears. I was completely rocked at the recognition of how powerfully this program was running me and yet I'd had no idea!'

This is typical of another way in which affirmations are dynamic — things often get worse at first, because the affirmation is drawing our attention to the problem it is aimed at. The crucial thing here is not to give up and drop the affirmation — it is working. Go with it. Let's look at where it took Jason.

Step 7
Using physical energy to free ourselves

Jason continued his story. 'Finally I got so angry, I started screaming back in my head at the negative self-talk, "Shut up! I am intelligent and capable!" Wednesday night I went home so hyped up I just had to do something physical. So I threw on my joggers and ran along the beach. I started yelling as I ran, hurling abuse at this crippling belief I'd taken on. I could see Dad innocently saying to me, "There, there, Dummy!" So I started telling his image in my mind, "It's not true, Dad! Don't talk to me like that! Stop now! Just STOP! I know you don't mean it and you're just trying to comfort me in your own way, but you simply mustn't do this any more!"

'The maddest thing happened — I could see his face crumple, and the image saying to me, "I'm terribly sorry! I had no idea — I just didn't realise you'd be taking it seriously". "Well I was!" I murmured, dropping my voice a few decibels and my furious jog to a walk. He continued, "It's not true, you know. You were such a bright little boy — always asking questions, looking for answers". By now, I had stopped running and was on my knees in the sand. There was just me and the ocean and the sky, and I experienced a moment of supreme joy, the exquisite joy of breaking out of prison. It was actually very spiritual. I felt enormous compassion and love for my father, and went home to phone him, just to tell him what a great guy he was. I think it was one of the highlights of his life, too.'

People have reported similar experiences of breaking free of old beliefs after their parents were dead, and experiencing the same feeling of unbounded joy, accompanied by a strong sense of oneness with the absent parent, a sense of somehow having 'set my mother free too', in Gina's words.

To be free of our limiting beliefs and the uncomfortable emotions they cause, we must permit the child-within to express whatever she was once not free to express. We simply have to allow her to 'answer back' verbally, and to hurl some energy against the energy invested in her limiting beliefs.

To be free of our limiting beliefs it is necessary to assert oneself over them, energetically.

In the course we spend a day doing this vital work. Here are some suggestions for ways of doing this yourself. Whichever way you choose, it is essential that you use your voice, aloud, at the same time.

For many of these processes you can use music to help you — something powerful and energetic. Here are some ways of going about your energy work.

It is saying the things we were never able to say that sets us free.

Take your list of limiting beliefs from Part Three, and an old phone book. As you read each belief aloud, shred pages from the phone book, representing the tearing up of that belief. It is important that you use your voice throughout this exercise, so keep talking to yourself about what you are doing as you do it.

Put on your favourite wild music and dance, dance, dance to it — all the while using your voice against your limiting beliefs.

Engage in your favourite sport, alone or with a friend who is in on what you are planning. Recall each limiting belief, or have your friend call them to you, one at a time, giving yourself time to respond vocally and energetically. Tennis, jogging and power walking are good for this exercise.

If you are a person who has easy access to your anger, you could kick and throw the phone book around an appropriate space. You could even get a tennis racquet, cricket or baseball bat or stick and belt the phone book or your bed. Again, use your voice throughout this exercise and some energetic music.

Set aside a time when you take yourself off to a remote spot with your beliefs list and let your head go — anything is OK as long as you don't hurt yourself or others or destroy property. Yell. Run. Stomp. Whatever, as long as you are consciously hurling energy at your limiting beliefs program.

You can probably come up with other ways to hurl some focussed energy at your total limiting beliefs program. Go for it! Assert yourself over your limiting beliefs program energetically, at least once or twice.

As you work on individual beliefs, you may feel the need to release physical energy again, as Jason did. It is essential you be awake to this possible need within yourself and honour it. Your experience may be totally different from Jason's, so don't expect anything in particular to happen — just go with your own energy and let it unfold. Recall the different shapes the need for physical release took with Gina, Dan and Jason, and simply do what you feel the urge to do. It may be as simple as going for a walk and 'talking back' aloud at the limiting belief and the situation that bred it.

Whatever works best for you, do it — physically and vocally.

When your outcomes in life are not as you want
them to be, you can change them permanently if
you recognise that
your unwanted outcomes in life
are largely the result of your beliefs program ...

Then change
your inappropriate decisions, actions, re-actions
and communications by tuning in to, accepting and
flowing with your negative thoughts and
uncomfortable feelings,
using self-parenting and the energy of your
emotions ...

Which enables you to clarify and change
your limiting beliefs
using self-parenting, affirmations, creative
visualisation, physical energy ...

And to clarify and take responsibility for
your unmet needs
using self-parenting, creative visualisation,
appropriate action and appropriate communication.

Ongoing change work

If you are working to provide more structure and self-discipline for yourself, you will find suggestions for further approaches in Emma's story on page 42.

If you have found it impossibly difficult to contact your own emotions, your child-within, be guided by the suggestions in Dan's story on page 69.

If you often feel overwhelmed emotionally, pick up the phone and make an appointment with a therapist or clinical psychologist. Don't let negative thoughts about taking this step stop you. You are injured and in need of healing. If you had a broken leg, you'd go to a bone specialist. If you have an injured heart, go to a good therapist. Reach out! There is an answer for you, so don't give up till you find it. If the first person you try doesn't help, try another. As in all fields, some are better than others. Interview them — choose someone who has an open mind to various forms of therapy.

Personal growth is a spiritual quest, an urge in the heart of all human beings regardless of religious denomination, and one that when fully understood is at odds with nothing taught by any religion. It continues for as long as you live because your potential to know and to love is boundless and restricted only by your limiting beliefs.

Beyond this book

We would love to hear from you about your progress or your difficulties. If you would like information about the course on which this book is based, write to: People in Harmony, P.O. Box 847, St Ives NSW 2075.

Related reading

Abrams, J. (ed.). *Reclaiming the Inner Child*. Harper Collins, London, 1990.

Bly, Robert. *A Little Book on the Human Shadow*. Element Books, Longmead, UK, 1988.

Capaccione, Lucia. *Recovery of Your Inner Child*. Fireside Books, Simon & Schuster, New York, 1988.

Dyer, Wayne W. *You'll See It When You Believe It*. Schwartz Publishing, Melbourne, 1989.

Ellis, A. *Reason and emotion in psychotherapy*. 2nd edn. Lyle Stuart, Seacaucus, Minnesota, 1977.

Ellis, A. *How to live with and without anger*. Citadel Press, New York, 1985.

Jansen, D. & Newman, M. *Really Relating*. Century Hutchinson, 1989.

Jeffers, Susan. *Feel the Fear and do it Anyway*. Arrow Books, London, 1987.

Kurtz, R. & Prestera, H. *The Body Reveals — How to Read Your Own Body*. Harper Collins, San Francisco, 1976.

Lowen, Alexander. *Bioenergetics*. Penguin, Harmondsworth, 1975.

Peck, M. S. *The Road Less Travelled*. Simon & Schuster, York, 1978.

Pollard, J. *Self Parenting — The Complete Guide to Your Inner Conversations*. Generic Human Studies Publishing, Malibu, California, 1987.

Roberts, Jane. *The Nature of Personal Reality*. Prentice-Hall, London, 1974.

Seligman, M. *Learned Optimism*. Alfred Knopf, New York, 1991.

The Self Alone

'I recommend *The Self Alone* as an insightful and thought-provoking book and a potential classic. It is not only the most complete collection of insights on the subject of loneliness I have ever read, it is also a positive and uplifting read — for every issue raised, there is a suggestion which will improve the reader's mental and physical wellbeing.'

PAMELA ALLARDICE, Editor
Nature & Health magazine

Loneliness is something we have all experienced, however fleetingly, in our lives. But are some of us more prone to feelings of loneliness than others? How do our early experiences affect our ability to cope with being alone in adult life?

The Self Alone explores the meaning of loneliness and provides insights into the experience. It encourages a shift in the way we view loneliness, helping us to use it to transform our lives.

Angela Rossmanith is a freelance writer and contributing editor in the areas of health, social issues and personal relationships.

CollinsDove
An imprint of HarperCollins*Publishers*

ISBN 1863714480